Jesus Every Day

JESUS EVERY WAY

Jesus Every Day

JESUS EVERY WAY

a weekly devotional

LISA M. HENDEY

LOYOLA PRESS.
A JESUIT MINISTRY

LOYOLA PRESS.
A JESUIT MINISTRY
www.loyolapress.com

Cover art credits: Neil Johnson/500px/Getty Images, zhen li/Moment/Getty Images
Interior art credit: RLT_Images/DigitalVision Vectors/Getty Images, youngID/DigitalVision Vectors/Getty Images
Back cover author photo: UCLA Campus Photo Studio

ISBN: 978-0-8294-6009-4
Library of Congress Control Number: 2025938419

Published in Chicago, IL
Printed in Canada
25 26 27 28 29 30 31 31 32 33 Marquis 10 9 8 7 6 5 4 3 2 1

To Greg,
my best friend,
every day and in every way.

Contents

Letter from the Author

Dear Friends,

Welcome to a journey of exploration and discovery! Seeking Jesus every day, in every way, has forever changed how I will live my faith. Whether you are someone who has been praying your whole life or someone who is skeptical about Jesus, I invite you to ponder Jesus anew: deeply, every day, and in every way. This book will help you do just that.

My parents gifted me my faith, teaching me from my earliest days to know and love Jesus, and I can't recall a day I knowingly skipped saying my prayers. My understanding of prayer is that this is how I communicate with the God who knows and loves me just as I am. But over the years, I found that too often, I was "doing" prayer as a series of tasks–albeit worthy ones–that I desired to complete. If I missed a part of my process, I derided myself. I don't say this to disdain traditional prayer. But in my desire to get prayer "right," I sometimes fell into the trap of going through the motions.

In undertaking the work of writing this book, I decided to set aside the tried-and-true morning prayer ritual I have lived for decades. My desire in doing this wasn't to quit praying, because prayer is my lifeblood. Instead, I hoped that by intentionally shaking things up, I could find a way to fall in love all over again with prayer, with freshness of spirit and hope.

So I suspended my normal rituals. I began to focus on the beautiful gift of encountering Jesus every day, everywhere I went. I had long been in the practice of daily time in Scripture, but I began to read it differently, keeping my heart squarely centered not only on the theological meaning of the passages but also on their intersection with my day-to-day life. I luxuriated over my Bible, lingering with it in coffee shops, at the library, and at my kitchen table. I also began to strive to encounter Jesus in the everyday stuff of life, those places where I live the many hours of my week when I am not sitting in church or my favorite prayer corner at home. Making these changes helped me to free myself of spiritual malaise. I found myself seeking quiet so that I could simply *be* with Jesus. Usually, no words were needed. Stilling myself to encounter the divine in the mundane set my heart free from needing to "do prayer" properly. I fell more deeply in love with Jesus, yes—but I also realized that this newfound way of praying is, for me, a transition.

The beautiful, centuries-old spiritual practice of *Lectio Divina*, which is Latin for "Divine Reading," teaches seekers to come to know God's word by praying over it methodically, purposefully, and slowly. In our world so full of bustle and distraction, it can be tempting to turn to our devices to help us pray with the Bible. But the prayer process of *Lectio Divina* asks us to set this aside and turn both inward to the quiet of our hearts and outward toward the object of our affection: God. This process invites us to

> withdraw, even if only for a moment, with the Word;
> read, listening intently;
> pause to reflect upon a word or passage that speaks into our hearts;
> dialogue with God or with Jesus, deeply sharing what the meaning of the word is for us; and then
> enter our lives changed and renewed by what we have read and heard.

For each of the Gospel passages in this book, I engaged in moments of *Lectio Divina* before putting any words on paper. Often, I repeated this interval of deep listening multiple times in different places. I adopted a new prayer practice: After poring over Scripture, I printed out the passage and tucked it into my pocket so that it was always close to my heart. Throughout the day, I pulled the printed passage out, placing myself alongside Jesus as I read the words again. By doing this, I could continue with *Lectio Divina* during my daily walk, at the hospital where I volunteer, in the front seat of my car, at my desk, or even at my favorite getaway spots, Disneyland and the beach. I let my mind carry me into the heart of the Scripture passage, exactly as though I were right there alongside Jesus and his disciples, no matter where I found myself. This change-up in the setting often prompted big, challenging questions I wanted to ask Jesus. It also helped me consider how the words of Scripture relate to what I call the "everyday divine" in my life, including the places where the beauty of Jesus's love for me had never really felt so vivid, tangible, and relevant to the ebb and flow of my days.

This book is a tool to help you seek Jesus every day and in every way. Feel free to read the chapters as I laid them out or pick a week that speaks to your heart.

There are five elements to each weekly mini-journey. First, I begin each chapter by offering a passage from the Gospels. Although the Scripture passages alternate between the four Gospels, they do not appear in sequential order.

Second are the personal stories about how the passage relates to the everyday ordinariness of my life, each shared in the hope that they will lure you into writing or pondering *your* personal points of intersection where the gospel applies directly to your lived experience.

Third, I offer daily quotations that strike me as particularly relevant to the word of the Lord. Some come from saints and Scripture, but most come from literature, poetry, and movies. I think you'll agree with me that encountering Jesus in culture offers unique benefits. Mondays feature a quote from a saint or "saintly" soul. On Tuesdays and Thursdays, we look at quotes from literature and notable writings such as speeches and letters. Wednesdays are poetry days, and each Friday is a Movie Night, with quotations inspired by popular films. On Saturdays and Sundays, our quotations come directly from the pages of Scripture. My hope is that these examples of finding sacred themes in popular culture will encourage each of us to keep our eyes and ears open for new and wonderful ways to connect with Jesus everywhere.

Fourth, I include in the daily reflections questions you can pray or journal about.

And finally, every chapter ends with a prayer. I invite you to pen your own prayer for each chapter, a prayer in which you direct words from the depth of your heart directly to Jesus.

My greatest desire for this little book is that it unlocks in you a sense of being held, accompanied, and cherished. I hope these words invite you to consider the everyday divine in the real life of your world—its messiness and its beauty, the moments of elation and the moments of sorrow. Please know that as I let this work go out into the world, I do so with a desire to walk this journey with you. Although we may never have met, every time I sat down to work on this book, you were in my heart. At each writing, I asked Jesus to send words to help you feel what I have been feeling. When you feel the need for human companionship along your journey into Jesus's arms, invite me along. I am active on social media @lisahendey but can also be reached through my website, www.lisahendey.com. Jesus gave us with all of our humanity to one another, knowing that we can best live his call to love and serve one another when we do this communally. Reach out with your burdens and blessings, and I promise to do the same.

In the early 2000s, my husband Greg and I checked off a mutual bucket list item when we purchased a 1974 Volkswagen bus from the son of a man who had recently passed away. We christened our treasure "Arnold" after its original owner, a mechanic who had kept it in pristine condition. Although we owned two perfectly reasonable cars, Arnold, even with all its finicky driving ticks, became our favorite mode of transportation. Arnold took our family on hikes, to the beach, and on all kinds of other adventures. When we drove

Arnold to church every Sunday, people shared our joy when they saw us coming. While our adolescent sons lamented their parents' choice of a vehicle that often left us stranded on the side of the road, they quickly understood that riding in Arnold meant seeing the world around us in a different way.

I thought of Arnold regularly while writing the pages of this book. Just like my current mission to encounter Jesus every day in new and profound ways, our time in our bright red bus taught me to live in the moment, to savor the beauty around us, to return the smiles of those who passed us on the highway, and to whisper copious prayers! Arnold is now living its best new life as a bright purple kombucha demo venue and influencer vehicle. But the worldview that quirky bus taught me has helped me realize that the divine can and should be encountered anywhere and everywhere.

So let's get ready to journey together. Jesus awaits us every day and in every way.

Blessings,

Lisa

WEEK 1

SUNDAY

Offering Our Gifts

The Visit of the Wise Men—Matthew 2:1–12

When they saw that the star had stopped, they were overwhelmed with joy. On entering the house, they saw the child with Mary his mother; and they knelt down and paid him homage. Then, opening their treasure chests, they offered him gifts of gold, frankincense, and myrrh.

MATTHEW 2:10–11

HAVING HEARD OF THE BIRTH OF JESUS, wise men from the East followed a star that led them toward Bethlehem. When they stopped and made inquiries in Jerusalem, King Herod summoned them, questioning them about their journey. Selfishly troubled, Herod sent them along to find the child in Bethlehem and return to inform him about Jesus's whereabouts. They ventured onward, led by the star. Arriving where the star came to rest, they laid their royal treasures before Jesus and worshiped him. Then, heeding a dreamt warning, they ignored Herod's command and returned home by another route.

Years ago, I penned a children's novel where my protagonists traveled in time to witness firsthand the Nativity story. In the story, my main characters, twins Patrick and Katie, met Mary and Joseph when they were traveling from their Nazareth home toward Bethlehem. The plot kept the twins close to the Holy Family through their flight into Egypt. I spent many hours praying and daydreaming with my young readers in mind, poring over the Gospel infancy narratives. I permitted myself to have Katie and Patrick's childlike vantage point. Meditating with the heart of a child, I heard the choirs of angels, the sheep bleating, and the hooves of the Magis' camels as they trudged onward, following the star in the Eastern sky.

Gospel commentaries point to the symbolism of the wise men's offerings. They bestowed gold for a king, frankincense to signify his divinity, and the embalming oil myrrh, a symbolic foretelling of Jesus's passion and death.

What gift will I give Jesus? I often asked myself while writing. The question has hung with me for years and is now part of my daily morning-reflection routine. Glancing over my schedule, I try

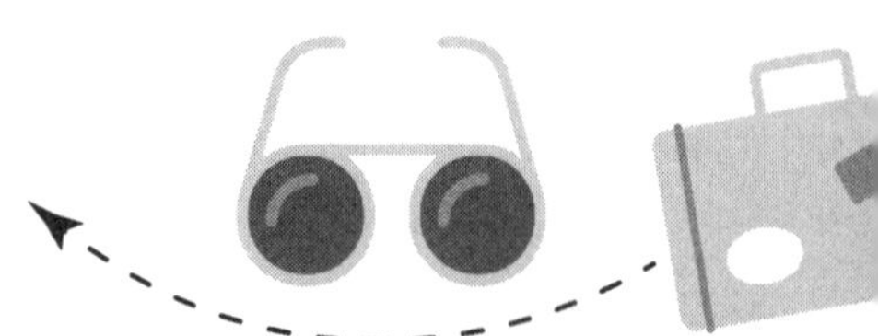

to imagine the moments during each busy day when I will have time for worship. Too often, this praise happens on the fly, in moments stolen between appointments and work.

But encountering the divine in the everyday stuff of life has helped me discover that life is a continual opportunity to bestow gifts on the King. When I consciously recognize Jesus's face in the countenance of those I meet daily, I am one with him. My gifts are a loving heart, a listening ear, and a creative mind. In sharing these with others, I lay them before my Lord Jesus.

My Sunday Reflection

What gift will I give Jesus today?

MONDAY

> But the love of benevolence makes our heart pass out of itself, and exhale itself in vapours of delicious perfumes, that is, in all kinds of holy praises . . . poured out to the glory of him . . . whom we can never right worthily magnify.
>
> ST. FRANCIS DE SALES, *TREATISE ON THE LOVE OF GOD*

How have I recently poured out my gifts for the glory of Jesus?

TUESDAY

> When you give someone your time, you are giving them a portion of your life that you'll never get back. Your time is your life. That is why the greatest gift you can give someone is your time.
>
> RICK WARREN, *THE PURPOSE DRIVEN LIFE*

Why is it essential to share my love for Jesus by giving the gift of my time?

WEDNESDAY

> Let God and the world know you are grateful. That the gift has been given.
>
> MARY OLIVER, "THE GIFT"

What is one gift I have received recently? How have I expressed my gratitude to the giver as well as to Jesus?

THURSDAY

> Gratitude is at the very heart of faith, especially for a believer. A Christian who cannot say thank you is simply someone who has forgotten the language of God.
>
> POPE FRANCIS, *HOPE: THE AUTOBIOGRAPHY*

How is gratitude at the heart of my faith in Jesus? Why does being grateful sometimes challenge me?

FRIDAY

> Then the Grinch thought of something he hadn't before. Maybe Christmas, he thought . . . doesn't come from a store. Maybe Christmas . . . perhaps . . . means a little bit more!
>
> *HOW THE GRINCH STOLE CHRISTMAS*

What creative gifts might I share with others to help them understand that Jesus loves them as I myself love them?

SATURDAY

> The point is this: the one who sows sparingly will also reap sparingly, and the one who sows bountifully will also reap bountifully. Each of you must give as you have made up your mind, not reluctantly or under compulsion, for God loves a cheerful giver.
>
> 2 CORINTHIANS 9:6–7

How might I give more cheerfully to Jesus and my loved ones?

Let us pray.

Jesus, King of peace, you came to us humbly, an epiphany of true love.

Accept the humble gifts I lay before you as a sign of my devotion.

As I seek your presence in my daily life, open my heart to give generously to those I encounter each day.

By loving them, I adore you.

Amen.

WEEK 2

SUNDAY

Today's Temptations

The Temptation of Jesus—Mark 1:12–13

The Spirit immediately drove him out into the wilderness. He was in the wilderness forty days, tempted by Satan; and he was with the wild beasts; and angels waited on him.

MARK 1:12–13

JOHN THE BAPTIST BOLDLY PROCLAIMED Jesus's coming and preached a baptism of repentance. Crowds gathered by the river Jordan to seek forgiveness. Among them was Jesus, sinless yet there to be baptized. As he emerged from the water, a heavenly voice announced that he was God's beloved Son. Then Jesus was immediately driven out into the wilderness to live among the beasts for forty days. There, Satan tempted Jesus.

Mark's account of Jesus's temptation is concisely contained in two verses. The evangelist omits the robustly presented details of Matthew's Gospel and gives only the essential facts. This sparseness provides ample space to place ourselves alongside Jesus in the wilderness.

Jesus prepared himself to enter his public ministry by going without food, protection from the elements, and companionship. He must have experienced brutal heat, blistering wind, and relentless thirst. Satan came to tempt Jesus physically and emotionally, offering not only bodily nutrition but also power and wealth. Our Lord, fully human even in his divinity, must have struggled mightily. But angels came and ministered to him, God's beloved son. He emerged, ready.

I live only a few hours from Southern California's desert spaces, and I have a deep love and a healthy respect for the desert. I know enough to enter that wilderness with a full gas tank, ample water, and sun protection. However, few places are as spiritually fruitful for me as those expansive vistas, where Jesus's presence feels tangible.

Our local deserts are now gathering places for makeshift music venues. The lure of earthly wealth, carefree partying, and easy companionship makes these events a hot ticket. Some things that tempt me mightily happen on those festival weekends.

But I don't have to be in the desert to be tempted. Influencer culture beckons me away from my real world into the promise of doing, wearing, eating, and living as everyone else thinks is best. Temptations come via my device, envy, exhaustion, or emotional hunger and thirst. In my weakness, I am tempted to click, follow, and consume.

But God never sends me into these moments alone. Jesus, who faced very human challenges and temptations that were placed in his path, walks alongside me. I, too, am beloved.

My Sunday Reflection

What is tempting me to forget how much Jesus loves me?

MONDAY

> For You, I sacrifice everything willingly. I offer you my body with all its weakness, and my soul with all its love.
>
> ST. GEMMA GALGANI

What weakness of body or spirit causes temptation? How can I invite Jesus into this struggle?

TUESDAY

> A silly idea is current that good people do not know what temptation means. This is an obvious lie. Only those who try to resist temptation know how strong it is.
>
> C. S. LEWIS, *MERE CHRISTIANITY*

Why is resisting temptation so challenging? What spiritual tools might help me?

WEDNESDAY

> I'd been tempted before, I couldn't be lured,
> I knew of the heartache and pain it caused.
>
> MARIA SHAW, "TEMPTATION"

When I was tempted in the past, how did loving Jesus help me avoid falling?

THURSDAY

> There is a charm about the forbidden that makes it unspeakably desirable.
>
> MARK TWAIN

Why am I tempted by things that are not good for me? How might I reframe these longings with prayer?

FRIDAY

> You're like the thief who isn't the least bit sorry he stole, but is terribly, terribly sorry he's going to jail.
>
> *GONE WITH THE WIND*

What would happen if I took my challenges to Jesus honestly and sincerely?

SATURDAY

> No testing has overtaken you that is not common to everyone. God is faithful, and he will not let you be tested beyond your strength, but with the testing he will also provide the way out so that you may be able to endure it.
>
> 1 CORINTHIANS 10:13

When has Jesus been faithful in helping me withstand temptation? How does knowing he is in my life give me strength?

Let us pray.

Jesus, you were driven into the desert alone, hungry, and vulnerable.

Yet because you knew your divine mission, you never gave in to Satan's lures.

Help me, Lord, when I fall prey to life's temptations.

May I always recognize that the riches that overflow in my life come from loving and giving myself to you.

Amen.

WEEK 3

SUNDAY

Loving My Enemies

Love for Enemies—Luke 6:27–36

But I say to you that listen, Love your enemies, do good to those who hate you, bless those who curse you, pray for those who abuse you.

LUKE 6:27–28

A CROWD SURROUNDED JESUS as he taught his followers to live counterculturally, choosing love over hatred of their enemies, extending mercy as God the Father does.

I will confess to having borne my fair share of grudges. Luke's Gospel describes many people who pressed close to Jesus, hoping against hope for healing from various diseases. But at that moment, instead of medicine, bandages, or ointments, Jesus gave them words: "Love your enemies." They didn't receive a quick fix. But they might have mentally flashed to someone they hated, or at least disliked immensely. That's what I do when I read these verses.

My idea of hating or being hated by an enemy transformed fundamentally following my travels to Rwanda in 2014. At that time, the country was nearly twenty years out from the horrific genocide when, for one hundred days, 800,000 Rwandan souls were massacred by ethnic Hutu extremists. As a writer on that journey, my work took me to various corners of the country to witness the Church's reconciliation efforts. Time after time, what I saw astounded me. Through mediated sessions, neighbors and community members were being led to forgive unspeakable actions of violence. I remain shocked by those scores of women and men who looked bravely into the eyes of their perpetrators and said, "I choose to forgive you." Their seemingly impossible interactions were active choices they often had to make daily, hour by hour. Some hurts are too huge to forgive only once.

Jesus teaches us to meet hatred with action. We are called to love, do good, bless, and even pray for those who have harmed us. My mother taught me that "love is a decision." Most of those against whom I harbor anger are blissfully unaware of my feelings. I tend to

hold my hatred closely, silently. Often, the person hurt most by my anger or hatred is me. Hatred is a toxin festering in me and seeping into every facet of my life and every relationship. But following Jesus's prescription—loving, doing good, blessing, praying—gives me a path to wholeness and peace. When we decide to love, we step toward the kind of change we may not even have known we needed. And we step toward healing.

My Sunday Reflection

Who is my enemy? Against whom do I bear anger or hatred? Why?

MONDAY

What we do not completely forgive, Lord, make us completely forgive; help us to truly love our enemies because of you; inspire us to truly pray for them before you; returning no one evil for evil; and may we strive always to help everyone in your name.

ST. FRANCIS OF ASSISI, *A MEDITATION ON THE LORD'S PRAYER*

If I choose to forgive, how will this help me help others?

TUESDAY

Forgiveness is the key which unlocks the door of resentment and the handcuffs of hatred. It breaks the chains of bitterness and the shackles of selfishness. The forgiveness of Jesus not only takes away our sins, it makes them as if they had never been.

TRAMP FOR THE LORD (movie)

How am I being shackled or limited by the anger I bear toward someone?

WEDNESDAY

Over the mountains
And over the waves,
Under the fountains
And under the graves;

Under floods that are deepest,
Which Neptune obey,
Over rocks that are steepest,
Love will find out the way.

AUTHOR UNKNOWN, "LOVE WILL FIND OUT THE WAY" (circa 1632)

What obstacles prevent me from loving my enemy? How will I ask Jesus to help me overcome them?

THURSDAY

> Resentment is like a poison we carry around inside us with the hope that when we get the chance we can deposit it where it will harm another who has injured us. The fact is that we carry this poison at extreme risk to ourselves.
>
> BERT GHEZZI, *THE ANGRY CHRISTIAN*

How has carrying resentment burdened me? How can Jesus help me relinquish this pain?

FRIDAY

> Okay, remember when we said that grief is the strongest thing a person can feel? Well, it isn't. It's forgiveness. Because a single act of forgiveness can change everything.
>
> *THE TALE OF DESPEREAUX*

What will change if I decide to forgive the hurt I am feeling?

SATURDAY

> Put away from you all bitterness and wrath and anger and wrangling and slander, together with all malice, and be kind to one another, tenderhearted, forgiving one another, as God in Christ has forgiven you.
>
> EPHESIANS 4:31–32

What first step can I take to ask Jesus to help me forgive someone who has hurt me?

Let us pray.

Jesus, you know every emotion that courses through my heart, even those I try to hide from myself.

I come to you begging for healing and peace.

Help me to lay aside my hurts and hatred.

For the one who has hurt me, I beg your blessings.

May they know the fullness of your love.

Heal my enemy. Heal my heart. Heal our world.

Today, I choose love.

Amen.

SUNDAY

Doing Whatever He Tells Us

The Wedding at Cana—John 2:1–12

And Jesus said to her, "Woman, what concern is that to you and to me? My hour has not yet come." His mother said to the servants, "Do whatever he tells you."

JOHN 2:4–5

MARY INTERVENED FOR THE NEWLYWEDS when the wine ran low at a marriage celebration. Jesus initially declined her request for help, insisting that it was not yet his time. His mother, who had known her son's destiny since he was in her womb, knew precisely what she was asking. "Do whatever he tells you," she instructed the servants. What happened next was indeed told in village lore immediately and forever: Jesus directed the servants to fill six jars of water to the brim. They did exactly what Jesus told them to do. Moments later, the wine steward credited the bridegroom for saving the best wine for last. The obstacle was overcome. Jesus had performed his first messianic sign.

When Greg and I invited my childhood pastor, Monsignor Michael Collins, to preside at our marriage liturgy, he had only one request: to preach on the wedding at Cana. Four decades later, the wisdom Father Collins (as he preferred to be called) poured out on us that May morning still overflows in our hearts.

"Weddings are fraught with obstacles, and the honeymoon is over too soon," he warned us in his lilting Irish accent. "Marriages have obstacles, too." Surely the bride and groom whose day had been saved by Jesus knew their fair share of daily trials, just like we would. "And here's my advice for you, dear Greg and Lisa," Father said. "May your days be spent *in* and *through* and *with* Jesus Christ. And with that goal in mind, please come to Jesus with all of your obstacles. Do whatever he tells you. Then your honeymoon will exist all the days of your life."

Father taught us to make our lives a triangle consisting of the two of us with Christ as our third side. He encouraged us to say, "I love you" to one another and Jesus often, but primarily when obstacles arose.

The triangle shape of a yield sign warns drivers to be alert to impediments ahead. *Slow down*, it tells us. *Take care.* Life is never without its obstacles. Greg and I have learned to yield to one another and Jesus, to slow down and invite his direction. And our love for each other and our Lord is like the finest wine: better with age.

My Sunday Reflection

What is Jesus telling me to do?

MONDAY

> Some of the greatest miracles of the world have similarly been done through the influence of a mother: "The hand that rocks the cradle is the hand that rules the world."
>
> FULTON J. SHEEN, *THE WORLD'S FIRST LOVE*

How does my relationship with Mary lead me closer to loving Jesus?

TUESDAY

> Faith is not for overcoming obstacles; it is for experiencing them—all the way through!
>
> RICHARD ROHR, *RADICAL GRACE: DAILY MEDITATIONS*

What is a past obstacle I faced? How did inviting Jesus to be with me help me in that situation?

WEDNESDAY

> With a lift of his chin and a bit of a grin,
> Without any doubting or quiddit,
> He started to sing as he tackled the thing
> That couldn't be done, and he did it.
>
> EDGAR GUEST, "IT COULDN'T BE DONE"

When I face something that seems impossible, what is my usual attitude? How might I be more Christlike?

THURSDAY

> When a person, yielding to God and believing the truth of God, is filled with the Spirit of God, even his faintest whisper will be worship.
>
> RON EGGERT,
> *TOZER ON THE ALMIGHTY GOD: A 366-DAY DEVOTIONAL*

Why is it sometimes hard for me to hear Jesus? How can I change this?

FRIDAY

> Happiness can be found even in the darkest of times, when one only remembers to turn on the light.
>
> *HARRY POTTER AND THE PRISONER OF AZKABAN*

If turning to Jesus in prayer when I face an obstacle is not my first inclination, how might I make this a regular practice?

SATURDAY

> You must understand this, my beloved: let everyone be quick to listen, slow to speak, slow to anger, for your anger does not produce God's righteousness.
>
> JAMES 1:19–20

When I am too quick to act, how might I practice yielding, listening to Jesus, and doing what he tells me?

Let us pray.

Jesus, your loving presence in my life overflows in countless ways.

Your signs are everywhere.

Teach me to turn to you first when obstacles arise.

May I come with trust, unafraid to ask for your help.

Say the word, Lord, and I will do whatever you tell me.

Amen.

WEEK 5

SUNDAY

Come After Me

Jesus Calls the First Disciples—Matthew 4:18–22

As he walked by the Sea of Galilee, he saw two brothers, Simon, who is called Peter, and Andrew his brother, casting a net into the sea—for they were fishermen. And he said to them, "Follow me, and I will make you fish for people." Immediately they left their nets and followed him.

MATTHEW 4:18–20

JESUS SPOTTED TWO BROTHERS, Simon and Andrew, walking near the Sea of Galilee. When he invited them to follow him, both immediately followed. Soon afterward, the brothers James and John also left their work as fishermen to follow Jesus.

Would I have followed him when the itinerant preacher walked up, extended a hand, and invited, *"Come after me"*? It's a question I've asked myself countless times. Would I even have recognized Jesus Christ if he approached me as he did his first disciples, in my workday life? Or would I have shot him a frustrated look for interrupting my train of thought, all too quickly turning my gaze back to my task at hand?

Most of us hope we would respond to Christ's call as Simon Peter and Andrew did, dropping our nets and immediately following without a backward glance. But this presupposes our recognition that a part of our hearts would be open enough to *know* our Lord somehow. It assumes we wouldn't just snap a quick selfie for our Instagram feed and move along with our to-do lists. Or, worse yet, cross the street to avoid the man altogether.

Although I call myself a lifelong believer, I fear I might miss out on the call I've waited for all my life. The thought of that possibility devastates me. So how can I cultivate the heart and disposition of one who responds *Yes* eagerly to Christ's invitation to follow him? Step one might be to open my senses more widely to the possibility of Jesus already being truly present all around me.

Jesus's touch, clandestine in the shaky hand of my elderly relative when I help her to stand and walk or the smooth skin of my child as I bathe him before bedtime.

Jesus's teachings, hidden in the pages of my favorite novel or the dialogue of a film I'm watching with my husband.

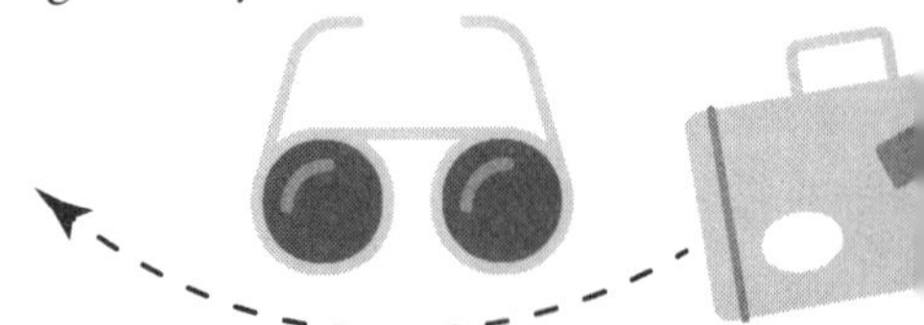

Jesus's call, camouflaged in the plea of my unhoused neighbor's request for spare change, or my partner's unspoken needs, the ones I'm often too overwhelmed to notice.

Jesus's Spirit surrounds us in our religious traditions and scriptural teachings. Still, Jesus is also to be found in those hidden spaces we too often miss in our introspection and busyness. It's time to lift our gaze, open our hearts, and be ready to follow the one who beckons us every day in every way.

My Sunday Reflection

How will I respond to Jesus's invitation to follow him?

MONDAY

If we wish to serve God and love our neighbor well, we must manifest our joy in the service we render to Him and them. Let us open wide our hearts. It is joy which invites us. Press forward and fear nothing.

ST. KATHARINE DREXEL

How am I committing my life to Jesus?

TUESDAY

To have faith requires courage, the ability to take a risk, the readiness even to accept pain and disappointment.

ERICH FROMM, *THE ART OF LOVING*

What might keep me from following Jesus in my life today?

WEDNESDAY

Follow me . . .
I will always understand.

ANNE CAMERON, "FOLLOW ME"

How do I believe my life will be changed for the better when I choose to follow Jesus?

THURSDAY

> When we come to Christ, we're no longer the most important person in the world to us; Christ is. Instead of living only for ourselves, we have a higher goal: to live for Jesus.
>
> BILLY GRAHAM

What are my highest goals in life? How will following Jesus more fully help me achieve these objectives?

FRIDAY

> Let me tell you something kid: Everybody gets one chance to do something great. Most people never take the chance, either because they're too scared, or they don't recognize it when it spits on their shoes.
>
> *THE SANDLOT* (streaming series)

Why is following Jesus risky? Am I ready to accept this risk?

SATURDAY

> Therefore be imitators of God, as beloved children, and live in love, as Christ loved us and gave himself up for us, a fragrant offering and sacrifice to God.
>
> EPHESIANS 5:1–2

How is my life an imitation of what Jesus taught and how he lived?

Let us pray.

Jesus, open my senses so that when you call me to come after you, I will heed your voice, drop my nets, and immediately follow.

May I overcome the fear, self-centeredness, and doubt that keep me from giving my life entirely to you.

Lead the way, Lord.

I will come after you.

Amen.

WEEK 6

SUNDAY

Living Our Sabbath Well

A Teaching about the Sabbath—Mark 2:23–28

Then he said to them, "The sabbath was made for humankind, and not humankind for the sabbath; so the Son of Man is lord even of the sabbath."

MARK 2:27–28

JESUS AND HIS DISCIPLES probably made a ragtag bunch, striding through the grainfields that Sabbath day. Mark's Gospel tells us that as they walked, they began to pluck heads of grain. The Pharisees walking with them immediately reported their misdeeds to Jesus. They were breaking the strict Sabbath laws, which prohibited labor. Jesus defended his hungry friends, referencing David and setting their critics straight on what would be a new kind of law and order.

It's taken me years to appreciate and embrace the beauty of Sabbath rest. While my husband and I have long prioritized worship with our faith community, we often bookended Mass attendance by running errands or fitting in extra work hours. I never believed that we were "sinning." But it was sometimes hard to differentiate Sunday from the other busy days of our week.

Our embrace of the Sabbath changed a few years ago when my mother-in-law was diagnosed with the early stages of Alzheimer's disease. Suddenly, instead of running to the hardware store or working in our separate offices on Sunday mornings before Mass, we drove forty minutes to her suburban home to spend the better part of our day with Norma. Since we typically attend Sunday evening liturgy, our Sunday mornings became oriented toward this family time. Now, we dine together, chat about the week behind us, help with her household needs, listen to music, look at photos of our grandchildren, and generally enjoy quiet time.

I'm embarrassed that my initial reaction to our Sabbath ritual was not very loving. While I care deeply for Norma, I begrudged the extra hours I'd come to rely upon to help me accomplish my overburdened work schedule. Having to slow down, "accomplish nothing," and just sit for hours on end was initially torture to me.

I now realize how much I missed in the years before Greg and I learned to Sabbath with love, back when stress, not renewal and relationship, set our agenda.

Now, Sunday is my favorite day. Our slower pace and focus on our elderly loved one and on each other is restorative. Our Sabbath rest and worship have become our greatest gifts, replenishing our spirits and binding us more deeply to one another, to the world around us, and to Jesus.

My Sunday Reflection

How do I typically spend my Sabbath?

MONDAY

> God is there in these moments of rest and can give us in a single instant exactly what we need.

ST. TERESA BENEDICTA OF THE CROSS

How is Jesus inviting me to summon a moment of Sabbath rest even amid a busy week?

TUESDAY

> If you keep the Sabbath, you start to see creation not as somewhere to get away from your ordinary life, but a place to frame an attentiveness to your life.

EUGENE H. PETERSON

How have I been keeping the Sabbath? How might I like to change this?

WEDNESDAY

> Six days of work are spent
> To make a Sunday quiet.

WENDELL BERRY, *THIS DAY*

In what ways does resting with Jesus on the Sabbath help me to love others more patiently?

THURSDAY

> Anybody can observe the Sabbath, but making it holy surely takes the rest of the week.
>
> ALICE WALKER, *IN SEARCH OF OUR MOTHERS' GARDENS*

What challenges my desire to rest with Jesus on the Sabbath? What preparations might I need to take during the week to Sabbath well?

FRIDAY

> God made countries; God makes kings, and the rules by which they govern. And those rules say that the Sabbath is His. And I, for one, intend to keep it that way.
>
> *CHARIOTS OF FIRE*

How does my understanding of living the Sabbath well extend beyond rules?

SATURDAY

> And on the seventh day God finished his work that he had done, and he rested on the seventh day from all the work that he had done. So God blessed the seventh day and hallowed it, because on it God rested from all the work that he had done in creation.
>
> GENESIS 2:2–3

What hopes do I have to embrace Jesus more entirely by the way I spend my Sabbath?

Let us pray.

Jesus, Lord of the Sabbath, thank you for calling me to rest in your love.

You call us not to days of rigor and regulation but instead to lives of refreshment and renewal.

Help me embrace the beauty of the Sabbath fully.

May my times of rest renew me to serve with greater abandon, energy, and hope.

Amen.

WEEK 7

SUNDAY

The Life That Happens as We Wait

A Girl Restored to Life and a Woman Healed—Luke 8:40–56

But he took her by the hand and called out, "Child, get up!" Her spirit returned, and she got up at once. Then he directed them to give her something to eat.

LUKE 8:54–55

LUKE'S ACCOUNT OF A MIRACULOUS HEALING and a restoration of life interweaves two stories about waiting. A synagogue leader named Jairus begged Jesus to help his dying twelve-year-old daughter. Jesus's intervention was delayed by a woman who had been plagued with hemorrhages for twelve long years. Not daring to approach Jesus, she simply touched his robe. Jesus immediately sensed her need and healed her, commending her for her faith. By the time he finally arrived at Jairus's house, the girl was believed dead. But Jesus acted, encouraging the grieving father to have faith. He took the child by her hand and fully restored her to life.

Life seems to be filled with waiting. In today's fast-paced world, most of us give in to the Pavlovian response to any delay and grab our devices. Whether we are in line, in traffic, or waiting for a loved one, we impulsively turn to our email, social media, or a game to help us pass the minutes.

Assessing the impact that "screen time" has had on my life, I've tried to take a hard look at my temptation to while away my waiting time by endlessly scrolling. I tell myself I'm being productive by multitasking, but the truth is that these moments leave me feeling empty and anxious.

During my cancer treatment, I experienced an oversized amount of waiting. My most cumbersome delays occurred in the Radiation Oncology department, where the waiting area was shaped like a circle. Donning our hospital gowns and waiting to be radiated, we patients looked across the room at one another while a screen on the wall counted down our time.

I made it a practice to stow my cell phone in the locker with my clothes for my appointments. Sitting in that big circle, I began a practice of praying the Rosary, using my fellow patients and their caregivers as my "beads." I didn't know their names, but it was easy to sense the immense weight they carried. Our waiting circle became my chapel. Delays became gifts. Christ's presence among us felt tangible. My six weeks of radiation treatment transformed my body, but more important, it transformed my soul.

My Sunday Reflection

How might I transform intervals of time spent in waiting?

MONDAY

> The patient endurance of the Cross—whatever nature it may be—is the highest work we have to do.
>
> ST. KATHARINE DREXEL

What cross am I enduring right now? How is waiting with Jesus a part of bearing this hardship?

TUESDAY

> Waiting is an art that our impatient age has forgotten.
>
> DIETRICH BONHOEFFER, *WONDER OF WONDERS*

How might I come to see waiting as a gift instead of a burden?

WEDNESDAY

> Time is
> Too Slow for those who Wait,
> Too Swift for those who Fear,
> Too Long for those who Grieve,
> Too Short for those who Rejoice;
> But for those who Love,
> Time is not.
>
> HENRY VAN DYKE, "TIME IS"

What is Jesus asking me to do with the gift of my time?

THURSDAY

> Once, when I was seeking the advice of Howard Thurman and talking to him at some length about what needed to be done in the world, he interrupted me and said: "Don't ask yourself what the world needs. Ask yourself what makes you come alive, and go do that, because what the world needs is people who have come alive."

GIL BAILIE, "IN GRATITUDE"

What causes me to hesitate rather than dive into what Jesus calls me to?

FRIDAY

> We live and we die by time, and we must not commit the sin of turning our back on time.

CAST AWAY

How can I see waiting time as a gift from Jesus?

SATURDAY

> But those who wait for the LORD shall renew their
> strength,
> they shall mount up with wings like eagles,
> they shall run and not be weary,
> they shall walk and not faint.

ISAIAH 40:31

As I wait with Jesus, how am I being renewed and strengthened for what comes next?

Let us pray.

Jesus, your love awaits me amidst life's busyness and distraction.

Help me to remember that the pockets of time I am granted are your gifts, destined to be transformed in ways humble and awesome.

Infuse me with sacred patience, to fully engage with the everyday miracles you sprinkle along my path.

Amen.

WEEK 8

SUNDAY

Multiplying Our Gifts

Feeding the Five Thousand—John 6:1–15

So they gathered them up, and from the fragments of the five barley loaves, left by those who had eaten, they filled twelve baskets. When the people saw the sign that he had done, they began to say, "This is indeed the prophet who is to come into the world!"

JOHN 6:13–14

JESUS SENSED THE CROWD'S HUNGER and asked Philip how they would feed them. Andrew found a young boy with five loaves of bread and two fish. Jesus gave thanks for the boy's meager staples and had the disciples distribute the simple meal to the five thousand assembled on the grass. Twelve baskets of leftovers were collected. The sign convinced everyone that Jesus had taken the lad's simple gifts and multiplied them miraculously.

When Cynthia and her siblings landed at the Honolulu airport at three in the morning in April of 1975, they were terrified. Their widowed mother, Đặng KimXoa, had shepherded them from their home in Vietnam, through Guam, to this dark place and an uncertain future. After descending the airplane stairs onto the tarmac, KimXoa and her children were wrapped in warm blankets. A Red Cross volunteer handed the weary mother a cup of hot coffee and a dose of hope for a brighter future.

The family ultimately went to Camp Pendleton, where they lived in temporary housing among fifty thousand Vietnamese refugees. Ultimately settling in Southern California, KimXoa found work as a seamstress. When her first income arrived, Cynthia helped her mother with a special request: The family sent a modest donation to the Red Cross to express their appreciation for the warm welcome they had been given in Hawaii.

KimXoa often remembered the impact of that single cup of coffee and the welcome and security it symbolized. Cynthia and her siblings witnessed their mother's generosity as her charitable giving continued. KimXoa used her blessings to help others, including family members who remained in Vietnam. But the photos of children helped by her donations touched KimXoa most. She recognized the importance of education and the hope it provided.

When Đặng KimXoa passed away in 2021, her children remembered how diligently their mother had worked to share her gifts with others. The Diep-Đặng KimXoa Charitable Foundation, begun with the $10,000 inheritance left to her children, was amplified with funding from Cynthia's volunteer dentistry practice. The Foundation now provides job training, educates minority ethnic students in rural areas of Vietnam, and funds a rehabilitation clinic near KimXoa's hometown of Hội An.

The gift of that single cup of hot coffee continues to bless others.

My Sunday Reflection

How have I shared a small gift to help someone in need?

MONDAY

> The important thing is to do charity, not to talk about charity. We must understand the work with very poor people as a God's chosen mission.
>
> ST. IRMÃ DULCE LOPES PONTES

What mission to help others is Jesus asking me to serve?

TUESDAY

> We cannot love God unless we love each other, and to love we must know each other. We know Him in the breaking of bread, and we know each other in the breaking of bread, and we are not alone any more. Heaven is a banquet and life is a banquet, too, even with a crust, where there is companionship.
>
> DOROTHY DAY, *THE LONG LONELINESS*

How has the act of sharing what I have with others helped me to see Jesus in them?

WEDNESDAY

> Every day you have less reason
> not to give yourself away.
>
> WENDELL BERRY, *THIS DAY: COLLECTED & NEW SABBATH POEMS*

What motivates me to give my gifts to others?

THURSDAY

> He who bestows his goods upon the poor
> Shall have as much again, and ten times more.
>
> JOHN BUNYAN, *THE PILGRIM'S PROGRESS*

How has the choice to act with generosity blessed my life?

FRIDAY

> All you can take with you is that which you've
> given away.
>
> *IT'S A WONDERFUL LIFE*

What is Jesus saying about times when I lack true charity toward others?

SATURDAY

> Some give freely, yet grow all the richer;
> others withhold what is due, and only suffer want.
>
> PROVERBS 11:24

Jesus multiplied the boy's humble gifts. How does he want to work a similar miracle in my life?

Let us pray.

Jesus, you gratefully accepted a small child's gifts, blessed them, and fed five thousand hungry souls.

Lord, teach me to share my gifts generously.

May I trust that even though they may be meager, your love will multiply them to bless those most in need.

Thank you for always feeding my soul.

Amen.

WEEK 9

SUNDAY

A Life Lived Differently

The Beatitudes—Matthew 5:3–12

"Blessed are you when people revile you and persecute you and utter all kinds of evil against you falsely on my account. Rejoice and be glad, for your reward is great in heaven, for in the same way they persecuted the prophets who were before you."

MATTHEW 5:11–12

SEEING THE LARGE CROWDS GATHERED, Jesus went to an elevated area, sat, and began to speak. He proclaimed eight beatitudes, phrases that considered a condition that is often viewed negatively, and did this in such a way that hope for the future is given. Finally, Jesus warned his followers that they would be reviled for their faith in him but that they should rejoice, knowing their reward would be great in heaven.

In the past few years, as I entered my sixth decade, I have actively sought relationships with friends outside my age range. Older friends' collective wisdom helps me understand the timeless nature of life's greatest mysteries. From my younger friends, I learn a flexibility that takes me outside the parameters of my traditional upbringing. My millennial mentors have much to teach me about living with authenticity and maintaining a healthy work-life balance.

Jesus's beatitudes, even taken outside their biblical context, are timeless fodder for good conversations with my elders and my juniors. This Gospel passage's countercultural feel speaks to the hearts of those unafraid to march to the beat of a different drummer. Committing to a lifestyle of love, peace, and humility beckons us to live lives that are dedicated to social justice.

I recently sat with a twentysomething friend and conversed about the challenges of living in our urban Los Angeles home with a "beatitude attitude." How might we move beyond simple steps such as lessening our consumption and toward radical solidarity with those in our community who daily go without shelter, nutrition, healthcare, and dignified treatment from others? How is it possible to live with pure hearts when so many images of violence, aggression, and mature themes hit us at every turn? How will we ever succeed at being peacemakers in a society where toxic polarization divides us against one another, even at our family gatherings?

Jesus never promised that living as his followers would be simple. He sums up his beatitudes with a warning that when we commit to living with intentionality, we will be punished. People will call us religious radicals, scoff at our priorities, or even shun us entirely.

With my friends accompanying me, and with Jesus and his example before me, I pray for the grit to live in a blessed (even if misunderstood) countercultural way. One day, it will all make sense.

My Sunday Reflection

How are the Beatitudes challenging me to live differently?

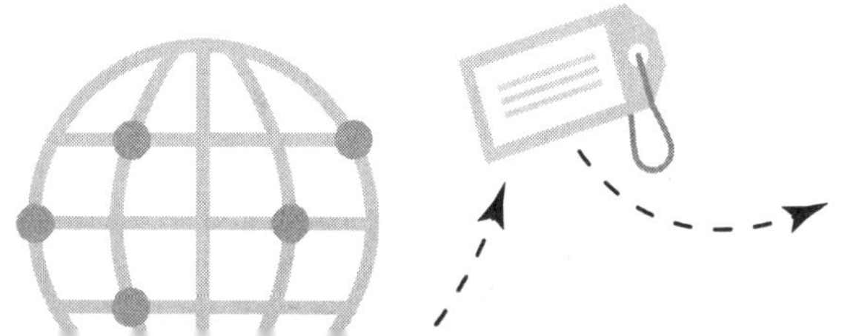

MONDAY

> To love God as He ought to be loved, we must be detached from all temporal love. We must love nothing but Him, or if we love anything else, we must love it only for His sake.

ST. PETER CLAVER

What earthly loves overshadow my love for Jesus?

TUESDAY

> Jesus makes it clear that the way to God is the same as the way to a new childhood. . . . The innocence that is reached through conscious choices. . . . The Beatitudes offer me the simplest route for the journey home, back into the house of my Father.

HENRI J. M. NOUWEN, *THE RETURN OF THE PRODIGAL SON*

Which beatitude speaks most sweetly to my heart? Which challenges me most?

WEDNESDAY

> Climb this mountain of beatitudes
> as you travel on life's path.

PATRICIA67, "BEATITUDE LIVING"

How has living with a beatitude attitude brought joy into my life?

THURSDAY

> I had always wondered why people never want to put a stone monument of the Eight Beatitudes on the courthouse lawn. Then I realize that the Eight Beatitudes of Jesus would probably not be very good for any war, any macho worldview, the wealthy, or our consumer economy.
>
> RICHARD ROHR, *FALLING UPWARD*

What is Jesus inviting me to consider when I pray with his beatitudes?

FRIDAY

> I feel like it's something God wants me to do. I can't just turn away from it.
>
> *GOD'S NOT DEAD*

What hurts have I sustained by choosing to love Jesus? How do I withstand this judgment?

SATURDAY

> Blessed are you who are hungry now,
> for you will be filled.
> Blessed are you who weep now,
> for you will laugh.
>
> LUKE 6:21

According to his word, when has Jesus blessed me for my choice to live differently?

Let us pray.

Jesus, you call us to know that our most significant challenges in this life will be our most beautiful gifts in the next.

Open my eyes and heart to the plight of those most in need.

Help me to courageously and selflessly choose accompaniment, solidarity, and even persecution for your sake.

In you, I have hope for the true love that lies ahead.

Amen.

SUNDAY

The Power of Story

The Parable of the Sower—Mark 4:1–9
The Purpose of the Parables—Mark 4:10–20

And he said to them, "To you has been given the secret of the kingdom of God, but for those outside, everything comes in parables; in order that

'they may indeed look, but not perceive,
and may indeed listen, but not understand;
so that they may not turn again and be forgiven.'"

MARK 4:11–12

THE CROWD THAT GATHERED TO HEAR JESUS TEACH grew so large that he took to a boat in the sea. He offered the people in the crowd the parable of the sower, a story symbolizing the impact of God's word in our lives. In the story, seed was sown on a path, on rocky ground, amid thorns, and then finally in good soil. Afterward, as he gathered with a smaller group, Jesus explained why he often employed parables in his teaching. Those close to him had been given a secret gift, but the stories were meant for people who did not yet have this insight. It was for these people that the seeds of God's word were planted into fertile ground to blossom, grow, and spread.

As the daughter of a gifted storyteller, I love a good tale. Growing up, Daddy often gave Mom a break by gathering the five of us for stories. Like the disciples, we also had our own stories and songs from Daddy, meant to celebrate some unique aspects of our personalities. Among our other storytelling traditions, I still treasure the faux-parchment-covered children's Bible we shared as kids. Inside this fifty-year-old book are tucked memories of my upbringing, including the shopping list for our traditional Thanksgiving dinner and the script from the Nativity play we performed for our grandparents every Christmas. Even now when praying over a Bible passage, I break out that well-worn Bible and remember the stories of our faith that I learned from my parents.

While I love studying theology, the homilies that have the most impact on me come from priests who employ the art of storytelling when breaking open the Word. I would have been among those people outside Jesus's inner circle who needed the power of parable to understand the deeper meaning of his precepts.

My Sunday Reflection

How has storytelling shaped my relationship with Jesus?

MONDAY

> Oh, mighty secrets of God! Never should I weary of trying to explain them if I thought it possible to succeed! I would write a thousand foolish things that one might be to the point, if only it might make us praise God more.
>
> ST. TERESA OF AVILA, *THE INTERIOR CASTLE*

How does the way I tell my story draw others into loving Jesus?

TUESDAY

> The purpose of a storyteller is not to tell you how to think, but to give you questions to think upon.
>
> BRANDON SANDERSON, *THE WAY OF KINGS*

What questions do I have about Jesus? Where might I go to seek answers?

WEDNESDAY

> Here we are, on our path.
> Let me understand you.
>
> JAMES WRIGHT, "LOVE SONG TO A MORNING"

What stories of faith shared by others have touched my heart and helped me to love Jesus?

THURSDAY

> Stories have to be told or they die, and when they die, we can't remember who we are or why we're here.
>
> SUE MONK KIDD, *THE SECRET LIFE OF BEES*

Why do stories about Jesus touch me?

FRIDAY

> It was his story against mine, but of course, I told my story better.
>
> *IN A LONELY PLACE*

When was the last time I shared a story about Jesus with someone? What happened?

SATURDAY

> You yourselves are our letter, written on our hearts, to be known and read by all; and you show that you are a letter of Christ, prepared by us, written not with ink but with the Spirit of the living God, not on tablets of stone but on tablets of human hearts.
>
> 2 CORINTHIANS 3:2–3

How is my life story a testament to Jesus's love?

Let us pray.

Jesus, master storyteller, you sowed seeds of love, faith, and trust into the hearts of seekers through the parables you shared.

Send me as your storyteller.

Enflame in my mind the heart of your gospel.

Open my ears to hear your word and my mouth to proclaim your love in new ways.

Amen.

WEEK 11

SUNDAY

Noticing My Neighbor in Need

The Parable of the Good Samaritan—Luke 10:25–37

But a Samaritan while traveling came near him; and when he saw him, he was moved with pity. He went to him and bandaged his wounds, having poured oil and wine on them. Then he put him on his own animal, brought him to an inn, and took care of him.

LUKE 10:33–34

A LAWYER TESTED JESUS, hoping to show his worth. Jesus shared a parable underscoring that loving and serving our neighbors hands-on is the ultimate way to show our love for God.

One day my travels took me to La Romano, a large city in the Dominican Republic. Gregarious Moises greeted my group at the sizeable nonprofit hospital where he serves as chief executive officer. Fundación Hospital General el Buen Samaritano (Good Samaritan Hospital Foundation) was founded to serve anyone needing medical care, regardless of their ability to pay.

What touched me most that morning was not the impressive array of care provided to the region's poor. It was Moises's story. Born in La Romana to Haitian immigrant parents, Moises beat the odds and parlayed his education into a life devoted to serving others.

Next our bus took us to a mobile medical clinic at Batey La Pinita. Bateyes, like the one where Moises was raised, are communal settlements adjacent to sugar-cane plantations and mills. The Batey is home to many families, mostly immigrants from Haiti, who come to labor in the fields. At the Batey clinic, various free healthcare services were underway courtesy of an American physician and her team of volunteers.

Shortly after leaving the clinic, we stopped on the side of the road by a sugar-cane field. The crops, six-foot-tall brown stalks, stretched for miles. A group of workers approached atop a large cart pulled by a team of massive cattle. The men shared their lives in the fields and the Batey, with Moises interpreting. Each had fled Haiti in search

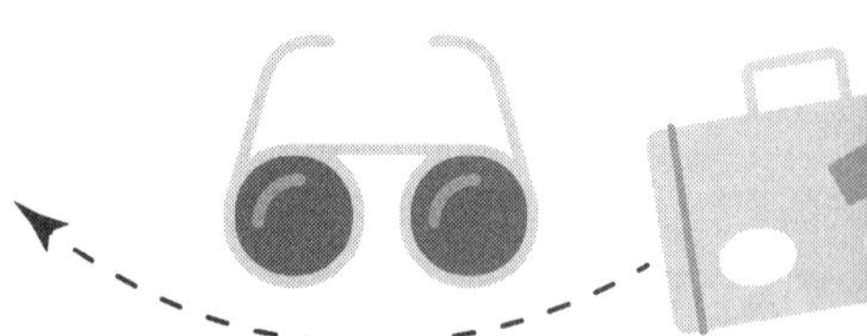

of work and hope for their families. They offered sugar-cane stalks, encouraging us to taste the dry sticks.

I'd never made the connection between the sugar that sweetens my favorite treats and the humans laboring to harvest it. I bid goodbye to the men with a lump in my throat and pain in my heart.

Moises, a modern-day Good Samaritan, challenged me that day. I must go and do likewise. Poverty and need exist in my community. Jesus calls me to see my neighbors, act, and show mercy with love.

My Sunday Reflection

How am I a neighbor to those in need?

MONDAY

> Justice at its best is love correcting everything that stands against love.

MARTIN LUTHER KING JR, *WHERE DO WE GO FROM HERE?*

How does Jesus invite me to show love and mercy by standing up for what he teaches me?

TUESDAY

> On the one hand, we are called to play the Good Samaritan on life's roadside, but that will be only an initial act. One day we must come to see that the whole Jericho Road must be transformed so that men and women will not be constantly beaten and robbed as they make their journey on life's highway. True compassion is more than flinging a coin to a beggar. It comes to see that an edifice which produces beggars needs restructuring.

MARTIN LUTHER KING JR.,
"BEYOND VIETNAM: A TIME TO BREAK SILENCE" (speech)

What might I do to further systemic changes to support those in need?

WEDNESDAY

> He passes through the city streets
> Unnoticed and unknown,
> He helps the sinner that he meets—
> His sorrows are his own.

HENRY LAWSON, "THE GOOD SAMARITAN"

When did I give generously but quietly? How did this bring me closer to Jesus?

THURSDAY

> Deep wounds are not easily healed. But the Good Samaritan poured oil and wine into the wounds of the stranger who lay helpless on the road to Jericho, and set him on the road to recovery. Each one of us can go and do likewise.

JOHN LAFARGE, SJ, *THE CATHOLIC VIEWPOINT ON RACE RELATIONS*

Where are the places Jesus calls me to give as the Samaritan did?

FRIDAY

> When it all comes down to it, life isn't about how much we get—it's about how much we share.

GOOD DEEDS

Why will an act of selfless giving help me connect more deeply with Jesus?

SATURDAY

> In all this I have given you an example that by such work we must support the weak, remembering the words of the Lord Jesus, for he himself said, "It is more blessed to give than to receive."

ACTS 20:35

What changes can I make to live more actively with my neighbors in need?

Let us pray.

Jesus, your stories point to the love you desire us to show one another.

There is so much hurt, pain, and need in my community.

At times, I feel too overwhelmed to know how to act.

Help me, Lord, to see the small ways you call me to be a neighbor.

Open my heart to respond fearlessly, with love and mercy.

Amen.

WEEK 12

SUNDAY

Life-Giving Bread

The Bread from Heaven—John 6:22–59

I am the bread of life. Your ancestors ate the manna in the wilderness, and they died. This is the bread that comes down from heaven, so that one may eat of it and not die. I am the living bread that came down from heaven. Whoever eats of this bread will live forever; and the bread that I will give for the life of the world is my flesh.

JOHN 6:48–51

THE CROWDS WENT TO CAPERNAUM, seeking Jesus. Since he had previously fed them, they again asked for a sign. He boldly proclaimed, "I am the bread of life." Declaring his oneness with God, he promised them eternal life through the gift of his flesh and blood. Unlike the manna from heaven that had been sent to their forebears, Jesus provided a way to unite eternally with him and his Father.

I have had the great blessing of attending Mass and receiving the Eucharist in hundreds of churches worldwide. One gift of our faith is its universality. Whether Mass is offered in English, Swahili, Tagalog, or Spanish, I may not recognize the exact words, but I understand what is happening on the altar. That same gift of everlasting life that Jesus offered to the emotionally, spiritually, and physically hungry crowds in Capernaum is given to me every time I receive the Eucharist.

I've spent a lifetime wrestling with the theological precepts of Jesus's "True Presence" in the Eucharist. Intellectually, I cannot explain or truly understand transubstantiation, the mystery by which the bread and wine become the body and blood of Christ at the moment of the consecration. When my need to understand overpowers my desire to gratefully accept this gift, my prayer echoes that of the father in the Gospel of Mark, who begged healing for his child, saying, "Lord, I believe; help my unbelief!"

I believe Jesus continually offers himself to me as a free act of love. I believe that along with the many other ways Jesus is intimately present with me in my life, he beckons me to the Eucharistic table and offers me perfect solace. I believe that Jesus desires to fill the empty spaces within me, the places where despair eats away at my being. I believe that when I am overwhelmed with happiness for the

greatest blessings of life, I can most intimately share my gratitude with Jesus when I receive him within myself at Holy Communion. I believe that the hungry parts of me that long for relief from life's stress, sadness, and burdens can only truly be fed by loving Jesus and accepting the gifts he gives me, which come to me without price.

For these reasons and so many others, I seek Jesus daily and ask him to live within me and nourish my heart, mind, body, soul, and my loved ones, too. Through Jesus, we are made whole.

My Sunday Reflection

How have I asked Jesus to feed me with his love?

MONDAY

> If we but paused for a moment to consider attentively what takes place in this Sacrament [the Eucharist], I am sure that the thought of Christ's love for us would transform the coldness of our hearts into a fire of love and gratitude.
>
> ST. ANGELA OF FOLIGNO

How has receiving the bread of life from Jesus transformed my heart?

TUESDAY

> All love craves unity. As the highest peak of love in the human order is the unity of husband and wife in the flesh, so the highest unity in the Divine order is the unity of the soul and Christ in communion.
>
> FULTON J. SHEEN, *LIFE OF CHRIST*

What has helped me to feel unified with Jesus?

WEDNESDAY

> All bread must be broken
> so it can be shared.
>
> MARGARET ATWOOD, "ALL BREAD"

Fueled by the bread of life from Jesus, how am I sharing his gift with others?

THURSDAY

The movement in our relationship to God is always from God to us. Always. We can't, through our piety or goodness, move closer to God. God is always coming near to us. Most especially in the Eucharist and in the stranger.

NADIA BOLZ-WEBER,
PASTRIX: THE CRANKY, BEAUTIFUL FAITH OF A SINNER AND SAINT

When have I sincerely thanked Jesus for the gifts he has given me?

FRIDAY

I love you. You complete me.

JERRY MAGUIRE

How am I made whole by Jesus living within me?

SATURDAY

When the Israelites saw it, they said to one another, "What is it?" For they did not know what it was. Moses said to them, "It is the bread that the LORD has given you to eat."

EXODUS 16:15

What are some of the ways Jesus is nourishing me with his love?

Let us pray.

Jesus, bread of life and Word made flesh, you come into my heart and feed the depths of my soul.

Draw me toward you, Lord, when the burdens of my life feel unbearable.

Nourish me with your love.

Send me to share that same love with everyone I encounter.

In you, we are made whole.

Amen.

WEEK 13

SUNDAY

Praying Alone and Together

Concerning Prayer—Matthew 6:5–15

When you are praying, do not heap up empty phrases as the Gentiles do; for they think that they will be heard because of their many words. Do not be like them, for your Father knows what you need before you ask him.

MATTHEW 6:7–8

JESUS CONTINUED HIS SERMON ON THE MOUNT, offering a perfect formula for prayer. He urged his followers to pray not for public exhibition but in private and with great humility. He gave them distinct words, stressing that they should hallow God's name, invite his perfect will, and ask for sustenance, forgiveness, and divine protection.

I grew up in a praying family. My earliest memories of faith happened in my local Catholic parish and our home. My parents taught me the concepts of "domestic church" long before I studied them in papal documents by gifting us a vibrant life of prayer and practice. We often recited the Lord's Prayer together. It bonded us spiritually and emotionally.

Over many years, I've been blessed to offer this prayer with others. Given its appeal across denominational lines, it is a devotion I can share with folks from other faith traditions. I've prayed it with members of our interfaith Bible study, on trips abroad in Africa, Asia, Australia, and America, and in the churches of Christian friends and colleagues.

I prayed the Lord's Prayer holding hands with Daddy and my sister Erin as we held vigil during Mom's last days on earth. Ten months later, Erin and I prayed it together at Daddy's bedside as he took his last breaths. As we prepared to lay our parents to rest, the words of this prayer they taught us first were on our lips and in our hearts.

I am amazed by the universal nature of the Lord's Prayer and its timeless relevance. These words Jesus spoke in his early ministry are a balm to those of us who are broken and longing to know the

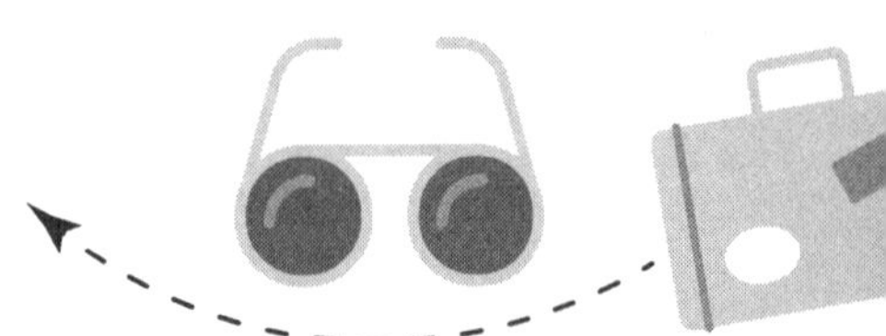

nearness of God's love. Though we've recited them thousands of times, we will spend a lifetime striving to live them with the trust and love which Jesus calls us to.

I most often savor the Lord's Prayer in the quiet of my heart. It reminds me that I am cherished, forgiven, protected, called, and sent by God, that I do not walk this path alone. Jesus, who gave me these words, takes my hand and leads me to his Father, who loves me and is always at my side.

My Sunday Reflection

What do the words of the Lord's Prayer mean to me?

MONDAY

> Thus, when we say: Hallowed be your name, we are reminding ourselves to desire that his name, which in fact is always holy, should also be considered holy among men. I mean that it should not be held in contempt. But this is a help for men, not for God.
>
> ST. AUGUSTINE, "LETTER TO PROBA ON THE LORD'S PRAYER"

How do I hallow God's name through my actions?

TUESDAY

> Father, make me a blessing to someone today.
>
> JAN KARON, *AT HOME IN MITFORD*

When has praying the Lord's prayer softened my heart to help someone in need?

WEDNESDAY

> We often pray God to let us have Truth.
> It is more important to pray God to help us live with it.
>
> ROBERT PENN WARREN, "WHEN THE TOOTH CRACKS—ZING!"

How can the Our Father be a lifeline and a pathway to the truth?

THURSDAY

Trust Him when dark doubts assail thee;
    Trust Him when thy strength is small;
Trust Him when to simply trust Him
    Seems the hardest thing of all.

LUCY A. BENNETT, "TRUST HIM WHEN THY WANTS ARE MANY"

What trust am I placing in Jesus right now in my life?

FRIDAY

Remember who you are.

THE LION KING

How does the Lord's Prayer teach me that I am in relationship to Jesus?

SATURDAY

The LORD is near to all who call on him,
    to all who call on him in truth.
He fulfills the desire of all who fear him,
    he also hears their cry, and saves them.

PSALM 145:18–19

Where have I felt Jesus hearing my cries and answering me?

Let us pray.

Jesus, you gave us the perfect prayer to seek and know the love of your Father.

I will hallow God's name and seek to be a part of the coming of his kingdom.

Come into my heart as living bread.

Forgive me for the ways I fall short of loving.

Transform me to do your perfect will.

May these words be ever on my lips and in my heart.

Amen.

WEEK 14

SUNDAY

Trusting Amid Rejection

The Rejection of Jesus at Nazareth—Mark 6:1–6

"Is not this the carpenter, the son of Mary and brother of James and Joses and Judas and Simon, and are not his sisters here with us?" And they took offense at him. Then Jesus said to them, "Prophets are not without honor, except in their hometown, and among their own kin, and in their own house."

MARK 6:3–4

JESUS AND HIS DISCIPLES went to his hometown and entered the synagogue to celebrate the Sabbath. He began to teach his neighbors, relations, and friends. Some heard and were astounded, but others questioned his worthiness to preach. Wasn't this the carpenter's son, the boy they'd known for years? Who did he suddenly think he was to tell them how to live their lives? Their rejection stung Jesus. He performed a few signs, healing some of the sick. Amazed by their lack of faith and refusal to accept him, he moved along quickly.

Sometimes, it's challenging to escape the boxes others place us in. We see ourselves in one light, but those around us may perceive us differently. This happens for all sorts of reasons. We may not be behaving authentically. Friends and family who have known us for a long time can often see through our false facades that can fool those who don't know us as well.

But most of the time, the evolution of who we have become is natural and true. We grow physically, emotionally, intellectually, and spiritually. That path may take us to entirely new places that are shocking or disconcerting to those who knew us as we once were. It can feel especially painful to be rejected because of our faith. Whether we've been lifelong followers of Christ or have only recently come to believe, some people may reject us for the creed we profess. This rejection stings most when it comes from those closest to us.

I want to walk alongside *all kinds* of people, not just those people who *like me*. Learning to lovingly and confidently navigate rocky relationships can be challenging, if not hurtful or bruising. But I'm learning to trust that Jesus guides my life. With some folks, love for

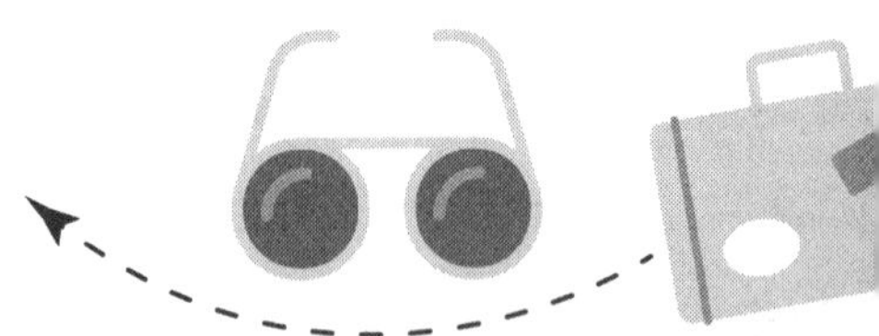

our Lord is a common bond. With others, I have to let my love for Jesus shine in different, primarily nonverbal, ways. This often means letting my actions speak, going the extra mile to see their perspectives, respecting their choices, and being a silent prayer warrior for their needs and well-being. Occasionally, keeping the peace means moving along quickly, as Jesus did that day at the synagogue. I pray in these moments for the trust and courage to persevere as he did.

My Sunday Reflection

How do I feel when I am rejected because of my love for Jesus?

MONDAY

> Actions speak louder than words; let your words teach and your actions speak.
>
> ST. ANTHONY OF PADUA, SERMON

How might people perceive me by observing my actions?

TUESDAY

> Self-rejection is the greatest enemy of the spiritual life because it contradicts the sacred voice that calls us the "Beloved." Being the Beloved constitutes the core truth of our existence.
>
> HENRI J. M. NOUWEN, *LIFE OF THE BELOVED*

When someone rejects me, what does this do to my belief that Jesus loves me?

WEDNESDAY

> If you can't be a highway then just be a trail,
> If you can't be the sun be a star;
> It isn't by size that you win or you fail—
> Be the best of whatever you are!
>
> DOUGLAS MALLOCH, "BE THE BEST OF WHATEVER YOU ARE"

Do I accept myself as Jesus sees me?

THURSDAY

> You can't go back and make a new start, but you can start right now and make a brand new ending.
>
> JAMES R. SHERMAN, *REJECTION*

If I have suffered a recent rejection, how might this be Jesus inviting me to a new start?

FRIDAY

> You see us as you want to see us: in the simplest terms, in the most convenient definitions. But what we found out is that each one of us is a brain, and an athlete, and a basket case, a princess, and a criminal. Does that answer your question?
>
> *THE BREAKFAST CLUB*

How do I see and sometimes reject others by looking at them superficially rather than as Jesus sees them?

SATURDAY

> Come to him, a living stone, though rejected by mortals yet chosen and precious in God's sight, and like living stones, let yourselves be built into a spiritual house, to be a holy priesthood, to offer spiritual sacrifices acceptable to God through Jesus Christ.
>
> 1 PETER 2:4–5

How do I believe I am chosen and precious to God through his Son Jesus?

Let us pray.

Jesus, I love you with all my heart, and I desire that my friends and family know your love, too.

Help me to compassionately navigate those relationships where my love for you is not accepted.

Let me never back away from what I believe.

But open my heart and my mouth to be a conduit of your unending mercy and care.

May my loved ones know you by the love I shower upon them.

Amen.

SUNDAY

Seeing Jesus in Our Brothers and Sisters

Jesus Visits Martha and Mary—Luke 10:38–42

But the Lord answered her, "Martha, Martha, you are worried and distracted by many things; there is need of only one thing. Mary has chosen the better part, which will not be taken away from her."

LUKE 10:41–42

JESUS AND HIS FOLLOWERS ENTERED A VILLAGE. Martha welcomed him into her home. While the hostess occupied herself with the logistics of entertaining, her sister, Mary, sat at the teacher's feet, listening intently to his every word. Martha spoke her displeasure to Jesus. Surely, he would see she needed help! Instead, Jesus reprimanded her, telling her that Mary had chosen the better path by cherishing her time with him.

Most of us reading this Gospel passage have asked ourselves, *Am I a Martha or a Mary?* Am I the type A personality who insists on making sure every detail is perfect, or the people person who thrives on the company of others? Most of us likely have both traits, but we also know ourselves and our families well. We're predictable.

As the eldest of five, I have some classic oldest-sibling traits. I am a peacemaker, a behind-the-scenes logistical helper, and—following the death of our parents—a family historian. Also among us is the bold law partner with a heart of gold, the middle child with the oversized sense of humor, the corporate businesswoman and culinary hobbyist who feeds our spirits, and the baby of the family, the tallest among us, who keeps us asking big questions. We each have our place in an unbroken circle. We live at a distance physically, but our hearts are proximate.

We five "B Sibs" (as our family text group is aptly named) have grown closer in the wake of our parents' passing. We are as varied as our occupations and living situations, but unbreakable ties bind us. It's not just the memories we cherish but also the new stories we are living that help us know we will always show up for one another.

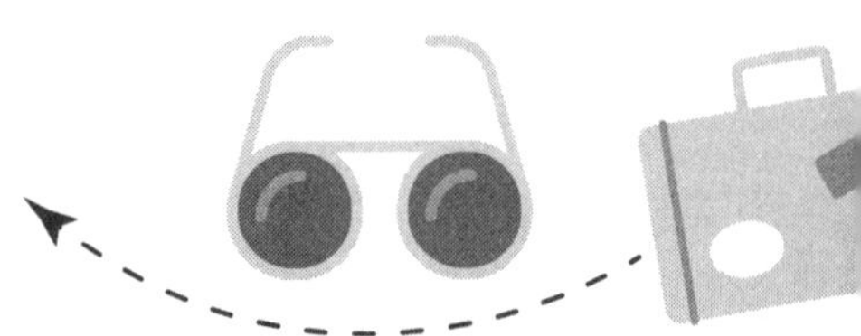

Though some of us experience our spiritual upbringing differently now, I quickly see the face of Christ in each of my brothers and sisters. When I ask them to lift me in prayer, the immediate support I receive, even from my non-church-going family members, is immediate and reliable. Our mutual devotion and presence in the best and worst of times is a testament to Mom and Daddy and especially to what Jesus taught those he called brother and sister: *Love one another.*

My Sunday Reflection

Who are your brothers and sisters?

MONDAY

> You don't choose your family. They are God's gift to you, as you are to them. Perhaps if we could, we might have chosen different brothers and sisters. Fortunately or unfortunately we can't. We have them as they have us.
>
> DESMOND TUTU,
> *GOD HAS A DREAM: A VISION OF HOPE FOR OUR TIME*

Who are the people in my life, related to me or not, whom I have chosen as brothers and sisters? Why?

TUESDAY

> Be nice to your siblings. They're your best link to your past and the people most likely to stick with you in the future.
>
> MARY SCHMICH, *WEAR SUNSCREEN: A PRIMER FOR REAL LIFE*

How have my brothers and sisters stuck with me during challenging times?

WEDNESDAY

> We cried together.
> We felt each other's pain.
>
> REBEKAH WALKER, "WE PLAYED TOGETHER"

Seeing Jesus in them, how are my brothers and sisters a reflection of the love Jesus wants for me?

THURSDAY

> I don't believe that the accident of birth makes people sisters or brothers. It makes them siblings. Gives them mutuality of parentage. Sisterhood and brotherhood is a condition people have to work at.
>
> MAYA ANGELOU, *CONVERSATIONS WITH MAYA ANGELOU*

How have I worked at renewing familial bonds with those I love?

FRIDAY

> We didn't realize we were making memories, we just knew we were having fun.
>
> *WINNIE THE POOH*

What memories of joy, sadness, and the love of Jesus do I share with my brothers and sisters?

SATURDAY

> Let love be genuine; hate what is evil, hold fast to what is good; love one another with mutual affection; outdo one another in showing honor.
>
> ROMANS 12:9–10

How do my brothers and sisters experience the love of Jesus by the way I engage with them?

Let us pray.

Jesus, thank you for the gift of my brothers and sisters, both those to whom I am physically related and those with whom I share a lasting bond.

Help me, Lord, to lovingly accept and support my siblings.

In choosing to cherish and encourage them, may my practice of the love you taught be perfected always.

Amen.

SUNDAY

Lighting Up Life

Jesus the Light of the World—John 8:12–20

Again Jesus spoke to them, saying, "I am the light of the world. Whoever follows me will never walk in darkness but will have the light of life."

JOHN 8:12

IN THE TREASURY AREA OF THE TEMPLE, Jesus made a bold proclamation to the people who gathered to hear him teach and the Pharisees and scribes who came to test him: "I am the light of the world. Whoever follows me will not walk in darkness but will have the light of life." Those looking to condemn him immediately accused Jesus of false testimony. But Jesus united his testimony with the testimony of his Father, God (John 8:18). They were one and the same. Jesus was not arrested that day, despite the furor he caused with his testimony, because his time had not yet come.

In Southern California, keeping emergency supplies on hand is standard practice. We are taught to be prepared for earthquakes, wildfires, and other unexpected catastrophes. My friends in coastal regions back East gather these supplies during hurricane season. In our emergency kit at home, among our other necessities are flashlights, fresh batteries, and matches. In an emergency, we will need to be able to see. Light is one of the most essential ingredients in our safety plan.

Light is critical to our physical well-being and emotional self-care. Many cultures celebrate the summer solstice, marking the year's longest day of daylight. Those who suffer from seasonal affective disorder experience depression that coincides with the shortening of natural daylight. Most of us take for granted that we can simply flip a switch to illuminate our path.

When times are challenging, we may describe them as "dark days." In these moments, it may be easy to forget Jesus's reminder that we will have the light we need when we walk with him. Perhaps this is one reason I instinctively light a candle during my morning

prayer time or why we time our Easter celebrations of the Eucharist with the sun's rising. The flame of a simple candle, or the dawn of a new day, draws my gaze and fills my heart with hope. My vision is renewed.

Jesus, God among us, promises us the way, the truth, and the life. It's up to me to trust that he will always illuminate my path toward him, even when I cannot see with my eyes. And when the darkness feels too overwhelming, I must remember to turn to my emergency preparedness plan. With Jesus in my heart, the darkness will never conquer the light.

My Sunday Reflection

How does a bright light remind me of Jesus's love for me?

MONDAY

> Don't let your life be sterile. Be useful. Blaze a trail. Shine forth with the light of your faith and your love. . . . And light up all the ways of the earth with the fire of Christ that you carry in your heart.
>
> ST. JOSEMARÍA ESCRIVÁ, *THE WAY, THE FURROW, THE FORGE*

How does the light of Jesus shine through in how I live my life?

TUESDAY

> Yet is it far better to light the candle than to curse the darkness.
>
> WILLIAM L. WATKINSON, *THE SUPREME CONQUEST*

When darkness surrounds me, what is one small way that I can bring light into my heart and into our world?

WEDNESDAY

> O star of strength! I see thee stand
> And smile upon my pain;
> Thou beckonest with thy mailèd hand,
> And I am strong again.
>
> HENRY WADSWORTH LONGFELLOW, "THE LIGHT OF STARS"

Why does the presence of light in my life give me hope?

THURSDAY

> So how, children, does the brain, which lives without a spark of light, build for us a world full of light?
>
> ANTHONY DOERR, *ALL THE LIGHT WE CANNOT SEE*

How can I trust that Jesus is the world's light when my faith is challenged?

FRIDAY

> Let there be light.
>
> *BRUCE ALMIGHTY* (and *THE BIBLE*)

When was the last time I asked Jesus to light my way?

SATURDAY

> For once you were darkness, but now in the Lord you are light. Live as children of light—for the fruit of light is found in all that is good and right and true.
>
> EPHESIANS 5:8–9

What does walking as a child of the light look like for me right now?

Let us pray.

Jesus, light of my life, open my eyes to sense your presence.

When my days are dark, help me turn toward the interior light you have placed within me.

In moments when that light is dim, enkindle in me the fire of your love.

Use me, Lord, to serve as your light to those around me who walk in a valley of darkness.

Your luminous love is bright enough for all of us.

Amen.

WEEK 17

SUNDAY

Why Worry?

Do Not Be Anxious—Matthew 6:25–34

Look at the birds of the air; they neither sow nor reap nor gather into barns, and yet your heavenly Father feeds them. Are you not of more value than they? And can any of you by worrying add a single hour to your span of life?

MATTHEW 6:26–27

PREACHING ATOP THE MOUNTAIN, Jesus offered profound truths to the assembled crowd. Among other teachings, he encouraged them not to worry about their material concerns. He pointed them to the birds and flowers, each cared for by his heavenly Father. Indeed, God knew and would provide for their every need. Instead of worrying, they should strive for God's kingdom and righteousness. Everything would be okay.

In the past few years, I have become an accidental birder. Friends chide me that this indicates I am now officially old. But I'm willing to put up with their joking because this pastime brings such joy. My birdwatching coincided with my cancer treatment. Stuck in a recliner for six long weeks following surgery, I opened a colorful book on birds sent by my dear friend Pat, a naturalist who carries binoculars on every trip and can readily identify birds at a glance. Pat's enthusiasm is infectious.

When my recovery permitted me to return to walking, I took what I'd read in Pat's book and avidly sought out birds. I was too weak to stride at my usual pace, and I needed frequent breaks. So I stopped, looked upward, and was delighted by what I discovered. How had I been missing so much beauty for so many years?

While I still have much to learn, spending time with birds has blessed me abundantly. Jesus was right about them, after all! Birds find sustenance, shelter, and relationships in what our Creator provides. Their lives are not without challenges. But the oldest known bird fossil is 150 million years old. The birds have found a way to evolve and flourish amid God's bounty.

My ability to worry less is another blessing that has come with my cancer journey. Worrying about an upcoming scan or a wonky test result does nothing to heal my body or soul. These days, when I am torn to pieces by something I cannot control, I sit with Jesus or invite him along for a stroll in our neighborhood. I won't say I never worry, but I am more content to let things sort themselves out.

Jesus is my daily companion along life's path. The birds, trees, and flowers that meet us each day testify that God, in his goodness, has a perfect plan for our lives and for what comes next. All will be well.

My Sunday Reflection

What worries me now?
Have I taken these worries to a conversation with Jesus?

MONDAY

> And yet never have I felt so deeply how sweet and merciful is the Lord. He did not send me this heavy cross when it might have discouraged me, but at a time when I was able to bear it.
>
> ST. THÉRÈSE OF LISIEUX, *STORY OF A SOUL*

What steps might I take to worry less? How is Jesus taking these steps with me?

TUESDAY

> If you're confused and praying to the Lord for direction, don't stop! Even if things in your life are looking bleak and it appears that God is ignoring you, keep asking!
>
> GARY ZIMAK, *A WORRIER'S GUIDE TO THE BIBLE*

When was a time that Jesus heard my worries and helped me?

WEDNESDAY

> In this short Life that only lasts an hour
> How much—how little—is within our power.
>
> EMILY DICKINSON, "IN THIS SHORT LIFE"

How might accepting that I am powerless over something bring solace and peace?

THURSDAY

> Worry does not empty tomorrow of its sorrow; it empties today of its strength.
>
> CORRIE TEN BOOM, *CLIPPINGS FROM MY NOTEBOOK*

How is worry blocking my relationship with Jesus? Have I listened for his presence in my worry?

FRIDAY

> I was amazed that what I needed to survive could be carried on my back. And, most surprising of all, that I could carry it.
>
> CHERYL STRAYED,
> *WILD: FROM LOST TO FOUND ON THE PACIFIC COAST TRAIL*

When was I surprised by my ability to cope with a challenge? What helped me?

SATURDAY

> Do not worry about anything, but in everything by prayer and supplication with thanksgiving let your requests be made known to God. And the peace of God, which surpasses all understanding, will guard your hearts and your minds in Christ Jesus.
>
> PHILIPPIANS 4:6–7

Have I ever been grateful for a hardship, and how did gratitude help me find peace?

Let us pray.

Jesus, you encouraged your followers to cast aside their worries and lean into the goodness of your Father's provision.

I am too often worried, plagued by situations I have so little control over.

Meet me in my anxiety, Lord.

Point me to the birds and the flowers and help me to flourish as they do.

Your love is sufficient for all things.

Amen.

WEEK 18

SUNDAY

Spotting Everyday Signs

The Demand for a Sign—Mark 8:6–13

The Pharisees came and began to argue with him, asking him for a sign from heaven, to test him. And he sighed deeply in his spirit, and said, "Why does this generation ask for a sign? Truly I tell you, no sign shall be given to this generation."

MARK 8:11–12

IMMEDIATELY AFTER FEEDING THE FOUR THOUSAND with seven loaves of bread and a few fish, Jesus departed for Dalmanutha. The Pharisees tested him, demanding to see more miracles. Jesus sighed deeply and questioned why they were always asking for signs. Refusing their pleas, he crossed to the other side of the sea.

I recently met with three women to discuss a project. We were newly acquainted and came from diverse backgrounds. Within a short time, it was apparent that we were "clicking." Each of us felt uniquely called and qualified for our shared mission. My colleagues remarked that the universe had aligned our fates. One called it kismet, while another said the universe had manifested alignment. Nodding, I quietly thanked the Holy Spirit for bringing us together.

I am, perhaps regrettably, not one of those people who will tell you, "Jesus told me to _________." I have friends who regularly report their divine allocutions. I don't doubt that Jesus audibly shows up in their prayers. But I have never been on the receiving end of a verbal message from Jesus. This might mean I should spend more time listening than giving our Lord my laundry list of concerns. Though I call myself a lifetime believer, my faith resembles a newborn's. My journey has deep chasms, sustained valleys, and brilliant hilltops. I am a work in progress.

While I'm not in the practice of asking Jesus for them, I have experienced more than my fair share of nonverbal "signs" from God. Two of these signs are dramatic, but I didn't recognize their significance until years later. Most signs Jesus sends me are subtle, not headline news experiences. Too often, I miss these quiet but divine moments in my haste and impatience. When I'm attuned,

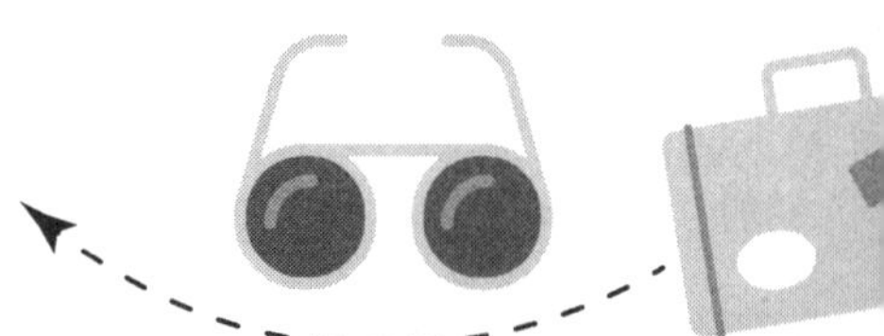

though, a perfect sunset, the symmetry of an ear of corn, or an unexpected text from a friend are simple signs that remind me how truly loved I am.

I have received tangible signs like the untying of a complicated "life knot" or the sense of a loving directive from my deceased mother. But I have stopped asking for overt signs. Instead, I ask for the grace to recognize and embrace life's most incredible miracle, Jesus truly present in the Eucharist. This should be the only sign I need. When I make it a practice to observe and give thanks for the daily signs of God's love, I suddenly realize how truly bountiful they really are.

My Sunday Reflection

When have I recognized a sign—great or small—of Jesus's love for me?

MONDAY

> You will find something more in woods than in books. Trees and stones will teach you that which you can never learn from masters.
>
> ST. BERNARD OF CLAIRVAUX, *THE LETTERS OF ST. BERNARD OF CLAIRVAUX*

Where am I most cognizant of signs that Jesus loves me?

TUESDAY

> In the faces of men and women I see God, and in my
> own face in the glass;
> I find letters from God dropt in the street, and every
> one is sign'd by God's name.
>
> WALT WHITMAN, "SONG OF MYSELF, 48" *LEAVES OF GRASS*

How am I a sign of Jesus's love for others?

WEDNESDAY

> Earth's crammed with heaven,
> And every common bush afire with God;
> But only he who sees, takes off his shoes.
>
> ELIZABETH BARRETT BROWNING, "AURORA LEIGH"

Why do I sometimes miss signs from Jesus?

THURSDAY

> It is a sign of spiritual health to be able to ask God every day to enlighten me, to recognize His will, and to have the strength to execute it.
>
> ALCOHOLICS ANONYMOUS, *DAILY REFLECTIONS*

How can I spot signs of hope and Jesus's presence when life feels challenging?

FRIDAY

> We're on a mission from God.
>
> *THE BLUES BROTHERS*

How is my daily life a mission from Jesus?

SATURDAY

> I have set my bow in the clouds, and it shall be a sign of the covenant between me and the earth.
>
> GENESIS 9:13

In which elements of creation do I encounter signs from Jesus?

Let us pray.

Jesus, giver of all good, thank you for the silent signs you send me.

Open my eyes to these unspoken gifts, especially when they feel hidden in my everyday busyness.

Use me to bear your love to others, especially those who doubt their lovableness and worth.

May your grace overflow in the tiny, the quiet, the everyday divine.

Amen.

WEEK 19

SUNDAY

Prodigal Priorities

The Parable of the Prodigal and his Brother—Luke 15:11–32

Then the father said to him, "Son, you are always with me, and all that is mine is yours. But we had to celebrate and rejoice, because this brother of yours was dead and has come to life; he was lost and has been found."

LUKE 15:31–32

A MAN HAD TWO SONS. The younger asked for his share of the family property. Taking his newfound wealth, he left and soon squandered it on a lavish lifestyle. Poor and alone, the son thought of his father's servants. He humbled himself, returned home, and asked for a job as one of his father's hired hands. Instead, his father rejoiced and celebrated his lost son's return. His elder brother, always loyal to his father, balked at this unfair treatment. But the father expressed his love for his elder son and reiterated his joy. What was lost had been found!

We pray with this parable and find ourselves in each of the three roles. We may be the father, lovingly extending mercy after being taken advantage of and rejected. We may be the older son, resolute in our choice to do the right thing but resentful when we feel slighted. Or we may have had our prodigal moments when our life choices took us far from how we were raised and our trusted circle of support.

Most of us can also look at our families of origin and cast our family members in the roles we see them portraying. But I wonder how some of my longstanding assumptions about the character of others keep me from seeing these people as Jesus does. I am that elder son, feasting on self-righteousness in my judgment of others. I am the prodigal, choosing the expedient when the long haul feels too daunting. I am also the father, standing on the hill awaiting my loved one, ready to wrap my arms around him and forgive everything just to welcome him home.

Jesus offers us a foretaste of what eternity promises in God's embrace. He urges me to give up my desires to control others, set aside my resentments, and beg those I have offended for forgiveness. I long for this heaven where the gulfs that divide us are wiped away and Jesus rushes to embrace us just as we are. But I also long for an earth where such love, mercy, and reconciliation happen *today*. Why wait?

My Sunday Reflection

Who do I connect with in this parable? Why?

MONDAY

I am the prodigal son who although I have squandered all the portion entrusted to me by my father, have not yet bowed the knee in submission to him; not yet have I commenced to put away from me the allurements of my former excesses.

ST. JEROME

How do I relate to the prodigal son? How is Jesus calling me home?

TUESDAY

Here is Christianity with its marvelous parable of the Prodigal Son to teach us indulgence and pardon. Jesus was full of love for souls wounded by the passions of men; he loved to bind up their wounds and to find in those very wounds the balm which should heal them.

ALEXANDRE DUMAS-FILS, *LA DAME AUX CAMÉLIAS*

Which of my wounds is Jesus binding up with his love?

WEDNESDAY

Fall down on your knees,
And say in your heart:
I will arise and go to my Father.

JAMES WELDON JOHNSON, "THE PRODIGAL SON"

From whom do I need to beg forgiveness? How will I ask Jesus to help me?

THURSDAY

> On the one hand, God is a God of justice who punished Israel for her wayward deeds, and on the other hand, he is a forgiving father whose heart was filled with unutterable joy when the prodigal returned home.
>
> MARTIN LUTHER KING JR., *STRENGTH TO LOVE*

When have I hesitated to ask God for forgiveness? How did waiting hurt me?

FRIDAY

> I know what I have to do, but going back means I'll have to face my past. I've been running from it for so long.
>
> *THE LION KING*

What parts of my past does Jesus want to heal?

SATURDAY

> Bear with one another and, if anyone has a complaint against another, forgive each other; just as the Lord has forgiven you, so you also must forgive. Above all, clothe yourselves with love, which binds everything together in perfect harmony.
>
> COLOSSIANS 3:13–14

When has the mercy of a loved one blessed me?

Let us pray.

Jesus, you remind me that even in my brokenness, mercy is mine for the asking.

You challenge me to set aside petty resentments.

You invite me to step into the joy of genuine reconciliation and forgiveness.

Help me hold the hands of all my loved ones as I walk toward the fullness and beauty of your Father's embrace.

Lead me home.

Amen.

WEEK 20

SUNDAY

The Grace in Grief

Jesus Weeps—John 11:28–37

Jesus began to weep. So the Jews said, "See how he loved him!"

JOHN 11:35–36

JESUS WAS SUMMONED TO BETHANY, the home of Lazarus and his sisters Martha and Mary. His good friend was ill. Jesus delayed his journey, and those present informed him that Lazarus had died. Arriving a few days later, Jesus proclaimed to Martha that their brother would rise. Mary wept, lamenting Jesus's absence. He surely could have healed her brother! Asking where his friend had been laid to rest, Jesus wept.

I know the rest of this story. Jesus raised Lazarus, thanking his Father so everyone would believe God had sent him. Oddly, a single line of this Gospel passage most consoles me: "Jesus wept."

I have known moments of copious grief in recent years. My mother, fighting valiantly against the effects of Parkinson's disease, reached a need for critical nursing care during the COVID-19 pandemic. During her last year of life, Mom's only words were garbled phrases of her favorite prayer, the Hail Mary. When she passed away, I was at her side, holding her hand. Daddy followed Mom to heaven less than a year later, succumbing to Lewy body dementia. Somehow, both of our beloved parents, each only eighty-one years old, were gone. Our loss felt unbearable.

Even now, when I think about their passings, I cannot contain my tears. I know my parents are at rest. But their absence in my life remains a perpetual ache. I have learned to survive my pain with the love of my husband, the companionship of my siblings, and the compassion of good friends.

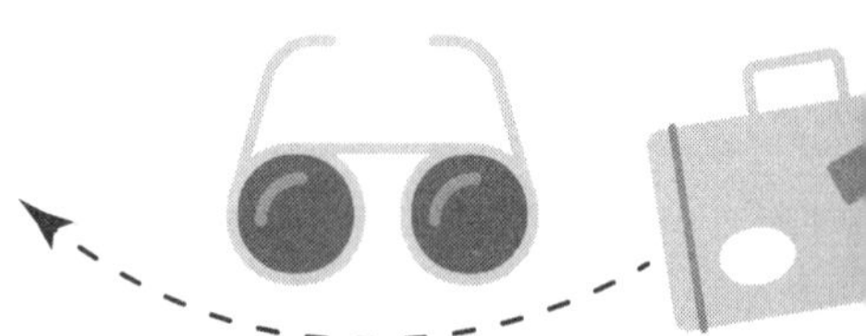

Despite this emotional support and therapeutic tools, my tears still flow easily. Folks have counseled me that grief is unpredictable. I have stopped fighting it, going gently with myself. And those two words of Scripture are often on my lips: "Jesus wept."

Jesus, who surely knew he was about to intervene on behalf of his dear friend Lazarus, gave in to what some call "the gift of tears." In my moments of profound emotion, I meet the One who is always with me and he bends my tear-stained face into his embrace. I don't fight the weeping now. Jesus is fully present in every moment of my life, and he weeps, too.

My Sunday Reflection

Where do I connect with Jesus in my moments of grief?

MONDAY

In serenity look forward to the joy that follows sadness. Hope leads you to that joy and love enkindles your zeal.

ST. PETER DAMIAN

When was the last time I grieved profoundly? Did joy follow that experience?

TUESDAY

I have withdrawn by myself, many times today, to weep. I have remembered Who wept for a parting between the living and the dead.

CHARLES DICKENS, *DAVID COPPERFIELD*

Who have I grieved in the past? How has their memory blessed me?

WEDNESDAY

"Where have ye laid him?" He asked. "Lord,
come and see."
The sound of grieving voices heavily
And universally was round Him there,
A sound that smote His spirit. Jesus wept.

WILLIAM MICHAEL ROSSETTI, "JESUS WEPT"

How does sharing my times of sadness with Jesus console me?

THURSDAY

> The personality of Jesus emerged from the Gospels with astonishing consistency. Whenever they were written, they were written in the shadow of a personality so tremendous that Christians who may never have seen him knew him utterly: that strange mixture of unbearable sternness and heartbreaking tenderness.

SHELDON VANAUKEN, *A SEVERE MERCY*

Why might being more transparent in my painful times help others draw closer to me and Jesus?

FRIDAY

> So you are saying I should get over my sadness by getting really sad?

NEVER HAVE I EVER (streaming series)

Where have I permitted myself to express sadness? Have I felt Jesus present with me there?

SATURDAY

> He will wipe every tear from their eyes.
> Death will be no more;
> mourning and crying and pain will be no more,
> for the first things have passed away.

REVELATION 21:4

How do I describe my hope for salvation with, in, and through Jesus?

Let us pray.

Jesus, you knew the depth of profound grief and shared your emotions, letting your tears fall.

Draw me near, Lord, when the sorrows of my life threaten to tear me apart.

I want to love as you did, but sometimes, this means accepting the pain of loss.

Gather me close when life's sorrows feel unbearable.

Dry my tears and help me to heal, serve, and love again.

Amen.

SUNDAY

Praying with Persistence

Ask, Seek, Knock—Matthew 7:7–12

Ask, and it will be given you; search, and you will find; knock, and the door will be opened for you. For everyone who asks receives, and everyone who searches finds, and for everyone who knocks the door will be opened.

MATTHEW 7:7–8

JESUS ENCOURAGED HIS FOLLOWERS to ask for what they needed, assuring them that his Father would hear and answer their prayers. He employed a potent example: a child asking for food. Just as anyone with a heart could not deny such a request, God is even more generous in hearing and answering our prayers.

Like many, I've often pondered this Scripture. Despite my optimistic nature, I can't help but be deeply affected by the suffering that plagues our world. Jesus assures us that his Father hears our prayers. But then, why do crises, poverty, illness, and war continue to afflict us?

I remember well the day I had a bit of light shed on answered prayer. Three hours from home, I met a good friend at the coast for a day of fun and friendship. We spent hours on the beach, then took a hearty hike up and down the coastal dunes. As the sun set, we said our goodbyes, and my friend left to head to their destination. I reached into my purse for my car keys and couldn't find them. Frustrated, I emptied the contents of my bag on the hood of my car. Then, I attempted to retrace my steps. I was totally overwhelmed by the vast sandy territory we had covered. There was no hope. The keys were lost.

I finally resorted to the one solution I knew would work. I called my husband. Just home from a long day at the hospital, Greg drove three hours to my destination with the spare car key. Then he caravanned with me through the windy roads back home, ensuring my safety. His impatience likely boiled over, but Greg never spoke about my carelessness. He simply helped me. I had prayed to God

to find my keys. God answered my prayers through the kindness of my husband.

Jesus urges us to ask, search, and knock when we are in need. But he also calls us to be followers who answer, help find, and open the door to the needs of others. We are called to be compassionate, to see hurt, and to commit to loving well. Most of the good gifts God wants to give us are delivered when we open our hearts, show empathy, and act with love.

My Sunday Reflection

What prayers remain unspoken in my heart and why?

MONDAY

> Pray to be ever ready for God's will, even when it takes you by surprise.

ST. MARY MACKILLOP, "LETTER TO THE SISTERS OF ST. JOSEPH," 1880

When did Jesus surprise me with an answer to prayer?

TUESDAY

> We must not shrink back passively. Our boundaries can only be created by our being active and aggressive, by our knocking, seeking, and asking.

HENRY CLOUD AND DR. JOHN TOWNSEND, *BOUNDARIES*

What restrains me from entirely asking for my needs in prayer?

WEDNESDAY

> Be thou the calling, before all answering love,
> And in me wake hope, fear, boundless desire.

GEORGE MACDONALD, *DIARY OF AN OLD SOUL*

How can my hope in Jesus draw me more deeply into prayer for myself and others?

THURSDAY

> Jesus tells us: "Ask!" and he also says: "Knock at the door!" and whoever knocks at the door makes noise, he disturbs, he bothers. These are the words Jesus uses to tell us how we should pray.

POPE FRANCIS, "THE BOTHERSOME CRY,"
MORNING MEDITATION, DECEMBER 6, 2013

When was the last time I "bothered" God by praying devotedly?

FRIDAY

> That question, "Where does prayer fit in today?", I'd say where does your heart fit in your body? Where does the air fit in when you breathe? It's an essential dimension in our very lives.

PRAY: THE STORY OF PATRICK PEYTON

Where do prayer and my time with Jesus fit into my life?

SATURDAY

> Rejoice always, pray without ceasing, give thanks in all circumstances; for this is the will of God in Christ Jesus for you.

1 THESSALONIANS 5:16–18

How is Jesus inviting me to pray ceaselessly for the things in our world that most trouble me?

Let us pray.

Jesus, thank you for knowing every need of my heart.

Help me in my fear and discouragement to have trust that your Father hears and knows all.

Open my heart to witness and respond to the asking, searching, and knocking of those most in need.

Your love knows no bounds.

In your perfect time, all will be revealed.

Amen.

WEEK 22

SUNDAY

Being Remade

The Transfiguration—Mark 9:2–8

Six days later, Jesus took with him Peter and James and John, and led them up a high mountain apart, by themselves. And he was transfigured before them, and his clothes became dazzling white, such as no one on earth could bleach them.

MARK 9:2–3

SIX DAYS AFTER REBUKING PETER for his reaction to the foretelling of his passion and death, Jesus took Peter, James, and John high atop a mountain. There, with his closest friends at his side, Jesus underwent the Transfiguration. His clothes turned brilliant white, and he talked with Moses and Elijah. Filled with fear, Peter suggested building memorials in the holy place. Suddenly, the voice of God announced, "This is my beloved Son; listen to him." As they descended from the mountain, Jesus instructed them to keep this extraordinary experience to themselves.

My mother-in-law has a framed printout of a humorous prayer hanging where she will see it each morning. Norma's prayer reads, "Dear Lord, so far, I've done all right. I haven't gossiped, haven't lost my temper, been greedy, grumpy, nasty, selfish, or overindulgent. I'm really glad about that. But in a few minutes, God, I'm going to get out of bed. And from then on, I'm going to need a lot more help."

I often think about the simple irony of Norma's prayer when I pray over the Transfiguration. How easy it is to be all that Jesus asks of us when the day is fresh and we've yet to make a mistake. All three synoptic Gospels tell this remarkable story of Jesus being wholly transformed. His closest friends watched as he conversed with their spiritual heroes. Given this foretaste of heaven, Peter spoke from his humanity. I would have done the same. Surely, some part of Peter wanted to stay atop that mountain forever. He, James, and John had witnessed Jesus transfigured, but then they, too, were forever changed.

It's often easiest for me to "listen to Jesus" in church. Having heard the Word and been fed by the Eucharist, I long to linger quietly in the sanctuary. The silence, sacred art, and lingering taste of Jesus's presence are tangible there. But like James, John, and Peter, I must come down from the mountain and back into the real world. As Norma's prayer reminds me, it's outside of my comfort zone that I must listen most carefully to Jesus. His transfiguration foretold not only his eternal glory but also the pain and suffering of his humanity. Like Peter, I'm not sure I'm ready for what lies ahead. But continual remaking in Jesus's image calls me forward. He is God's beloved son. I will listen.

My Sunday Reflection

How is Jesus calling me to be transfigured with him?

MONDAY

> By His loving foresight He allowed them to taste for a short time the contemplation of eternal joy, so that they might bear persecution bravely.
>
> ST. BEDE THE VENERABLE

When has knowing Jesus loves me helped me face persecution?

TUESDAY

> If you want to know, life is the principle of self-renewal, it is constantly renewing and remaking and changing and transfiguring itself, it is infinitely beyond your or my obtuse theories about it.
>
> BORIS PASTERNAK, *DOCTOR ZHIVAGO*

How is Jesus working in my heart to renew my love for him and others?

WEDNESDAY

> Because you exist I see it better, though the same
> as before.
> Because you love me I love it in the same way, but more.
>
> FERNANDO PESSOA, "BEFORE I HAD YOU"

Why am I willing to be transfigured out of love for Jesus?

THURSDAY

> Lament is a cry of belief in a good God, a God who has His ear to our hearts, a God who transfigures the ugly into beauty.

ANN VOSKAMP, *ONE THOUSAND GIFTS: A DARE TO LIVE FULLY RIGHT WHERE YOU ARE*

What woundedness or hurt in my life does Jesus want to transform?

FRIDAY

> Neo, sooner or later, you're going to realize, just as I did, that there's a difference between knowing the path and walking the path.

THE MATRIX

What is the difference between knowing Jesus's story and letting it transform me fully?

SATURDAY

> My child, be attentive to my words;
> incline your ear to my sayings.
> Do not let them escape from your sight;
> keep them within your heart.
> For they are life to those who find them,
> and healing to all their flesh.

PROVERBS 4:20–22

Where am I most able to listen to Jesus? What does that place mean to me?

Let us pray.

Jesus, beloved son of God, your friends witnessed your dazzling transfiguration.

This foretaste of heaven promised them the bliss of being forever in your presence but also foretold your Passion and their own trials.

Continually transform me, Lord.

Give me courage for the path ahead. Speak your words of mission and love into my heart.

I will listen.

Amen.

WEEK 23

SUNDAY

Caring Enough to Change Our Ways

The Rich Man and Lazarus—Luke 16:19–31

There was a rich man who was dressed in purple and fine linen and who feasted sumptuously every day. And at his gate lay a poor man named Lazarus, covered with sores, who longed to satisfy his hunger with what fell from the rich man's table; even the dogs would come and lick his sores.

LUKE 16:19–21

JESUS GATHERED HIS DISCIPLES and told them a series of parables, including one about two men who lived very different lives. The rich man dressed in fineries and feasted daily. The poor man, Lazarus, lay at the rich man's gate and longed for even a morsel of food. Both men died, but they experienced vastly different fates: Abraham embraced Lazarus, while the rich man suffered eternal damnation. When the rich man begged God to send a warning sign to his family, his request was denied. Jesus reminded those listening that enough signs had already been given.

I recently attended a funeral for Danny, a dear friend who for years has been like a second father to our family. A retired Marine, respected banking professional, and lifelong volunteer, he touched so many lives that his celebration of life literally overflowed with friends and family.

While Danny accrued monumental accomplishments, most who offered tributes to his life testified to the quality of his oversized, compassionate spirit. He accumulated financial security for his family but was incredibly generous with his gifts. His children shared humorous anecdotes and spoke emotionally of the loving legacy he had left for his grandchildren. Members of his faith community recounted Danny's giving nature and stewardship of his church. Friends shared the many ways in which time in Danny's company had blessed their hearts.

I walked away from the funeral service reminded of what matters most in this life. Danny garnered financial success but accumulated more of what my mom called "jewels in his crown in heaven." I drove home thinking about how little our résumés matter. The love we shower on others is what people most remember.

We shouldn't spend our days preoccupied with what people will write in our obituaries. Unlike the unnamed purple-clad "rich man" in Jesus's parable, Danny shared his wealth bountifully. The signs of what Jesus asks of us are all around us. In a world rife with material and emotional poverty, we must care enough to open our eyes and hearts to notice, respond to, and act on behalf of the Lazaruses we meet before it's too late.

My Sunday Reflection

What blinds me to the needs of others? What will open my eyes?

MONDAY

> I have my mission—I may never know it in this life, but I shall be told it in the next. . . . I am a link in a chain, a bond of connection between persons.

JOHN HENRY NEWMAN, *MEDITATIONS AND DEVOTIONS*

When did I offer a small gift of myself to someone? How did it draw me closer to that person and to Jesus?

TUESDAY

> No one has ever become poor by giving.

ANNE FRANK, *THE DIARY OF ANNE FRANK: THE PLAY*

How has being generous enriched me spiritually?

WEDNESDAY

> I know a man who thinks he's poor,
> But he is rich indeed,
> He has a chair, a friend who's sure,
> And three good books to read!

ANNETTE WYNNE, "I KNOW A MAN"

Who among my friends or family teaches me to be rich in spirit? Have I shared my appreciation with them?

THURSDAY

> If you're in trouble, or hurt or need—go to the poor people. They're the only ones that'll help—the only ones.
>
> JOHN STEINBECK, *THE GRAPES OF WRATH*

Where have I witnessed material or spiritual poverty in my community? How is Jesus inviting me to help these neighbors?

FRIDAY

> I guess it's hard for people who are so used to things the way they are—even if they're bad—to change. 'Cause they kind of give up. And when they do, everybody kind of loses.
>
> *PAY IT FORWARD*

How is Jesus inviting me to change something fundamental in my life to more closely align myself with his teachings?

SATURDAY

> Therefore say to them, Thus says the LORD of hosts: Return to me, says the LORD of hosts, and I will return to you, says the LORD of hosts.
>
> ZECHARIAH 1:3

When in the past have I "returned" to Jesus? What did this feel like and how did it change me?

Let us pray.

Jesus, Son of the Most High, you have given us the most excellent sign of God's will for our lives.

Open my heart to the poor around me, those who hunger physically and spiritually.

Use me to tend to their woundedness and to bind up their aching hearts.

May I always be rich in the things that bring me closest to you.

Amen.

SUNDAY

Accepting Help

Jesus Washes the Disciples' Feet—John 13:1–15

Peter said to him, "You will never wash my feet." Jesus answered him, "Unless I wash you, you have no part in me." Simon Peter said to him, "Lord, not my feet only but also my hands and my head!"

JOHN 13:8–9

KNOWING ALL THAT WAS ABOUT TO OCCUR, Jesus rose from the table and began to wash the feet of his disciples. Simon Peter objected. He felt unworthy that the master would lower himself to render a menial task for him. When Jesus clarified that without this washing, the disciples would have no share in his mission, Simon Peter swiftly changed his mind and permitted the act of service. Jesus encouraged all of them to follow his example.

I relate to Simon Peter's hesitancy when I imagine what it would be like for my Lord and Savior to lower himself before me and wash my feet. My embarrassment feels tangible. Like Peter, I would have argued with Jesus and perhaps even boldly instructed him that I should be doing the foot washing.

Living with others involves lovingly, sometimes begrudgingly, performing acts of service for them. Whether I am a parent potty training a toddler, a roommate cleaning the shared bathroom, or a neighbor tasked with pet sitting, being in a relationship with someone means cooperating with them for the greater good. In general, I'm a good helper. Some of my most blessed memories of my parents' final years were the times I could lend a hand by cutting Daddy's hair or pushing Mom's wheelchair. It felt good to be able to do something to soothe their suffering.

What's harder is submitting to being helped. When I was recuperating from my cancer surgery, I learned the challenge of genuinely humbling myself. My marriage to my husband spans nearly four decades, and yet letting Greg help me to the bathroom or bathe me were excruciating experiences. What helped me was to reverse the situation mentally and realize how happy I would feel to serve him in those ways. Looking back, I love recalling how tender the moments between us were.

Jesus urges us to be foot washers, but he also wants us to be people who are humble enough to allow our own feet to be washed. When I find myself cringing rather than expressing gratitude, I try to imagine Jesus asking if he could help me. Would I let Jesus brush my hair, reach for something on the high shelf, or explain a complicated problem? Absolutely! Willingly being on the receiving end of acts of service is its own kind of gift of humility. It makes us eager to reciprocate.

My Sunday Reflection

What is Jesus telling me about humbly accepting help from others?

MONDAY

> Let them never forget that humility is the source of all peace of mind; let them be able to put up with each other's shortcomings, because there is no perfection in this world, only in Heaven.

ST. JOHN BOSCO, "LETTER FROM ROME"

When did Jesus reach out to me through a loving act by a friend?

TUESDAY

> The mark of the immature man is that he wants to die nobly for a cause, while the mark of the mature man is that he wants to live humbly for one.

J. D. SALINGER, *THE CATCHER IN THE RYE*

How does letting someone help me make me feel? Would Jesus want this for me?

WEDNESDAY

> In thee compassion is, in thee is pity,
> In thee magnificence; in thee unites
> Whate'er of goodness is in any creature.

DANTE ALIGHIERI, "CANTO 23," *PARADISO*

Who is Jesus asking me to serve humbly despite my hesitations? How do I see the good in that person?

THURSDAY

> The Lord washes us and cleanses us of all the dirt our feet have accumulated in following Him. This is something holy. Do not let your feet remain dirty. Like battle wounds, the Lord kisses them and washes away the grime of our labors.

POPE FRANCIS,
HOLY THURSDAY MASS, ST. PETER'S BASILICA, APRIL 2, 2015

What acts of loving service have dirtied my feet yet drawn me closer to Jesus?

FRIDAY

> I'm here because I want to get better.

ROCKETMAN

What is preventing me from asking Jesus and others for the help I need?

SATURDAY

> Bear one another's burdens, and in this way you will fulfill the law of Christ.

GALATIANS 6:2

When has being served when I was suffering reminded me of Jesus's love for me?

Let us pray.

Jesus, you knelt before your disciples and humbly, lovingly served them.

It's often hard for me to accept help with humility and gratitude.

Help me to realize, as Simon Peter did, that your love sometimes comes to me through gifts and acts offered by my loved ones.

Draw me near, Lord, and wash my feet.

Amen.

WEEK 25

SUNDAY

Distrusting False Witnesses

False Prophets—Matthew 7:15–20

Beware of false prophets, who come to you in sheep's clothing but inwardly are ravenous wolves. You will know them by their fruits. Are grapes gathered from thorns, or figs from thistles? In the same way, every good tree bears good fruit, but the bad tree bears bad fruit.

MATTHEW 7:15–17

JESUS CONTINUED TO SPEAK to the assembled crowds, warning them against false prophets. He used the imagery of fruit trees and the goodness or badness that can be discerned by their fruit. False prophets would be cut down and thrown away, just like the trees that bore bad fruit.

Our nation regularly undergoes the rites and passages of our democratic system. During these years, we nominate, vote for, and inaugurate leaders who take oaths of office. But these are not our only leaders. We revere the athlete who has led his team to a national championship. We spend thousands of dollars to see our favorite pop star in concert. We listen to the opinions of award-winning actors and authors on everything from parenting to politics. Society has coined the term *influencers* to describe those who employ social media tools to advise their followers on the latest fashion, culture, and family trends.

With so many modern-day prophets offering their brand of wisdom, it's important to follow Jesus's advice and look at the fruits of their lives. Many of them are remarkable people whose talents exemplify an overall lifestyle of excellence. They develop platforms in their chosen arena but enjoy using this spotlight to bless others.

Unfortunately, we also often hear of the personal and professional disasters of many others. Like Icarus flying too close to the sun, they risk it all, and in the process fail themselves as well as those of us who have trusted in them.

Jesus is the one influencer we can always trust. His Gospel teachings are the fruit that points to the truth of what he professed. When we follow Jesus and act as he instructs, we, in turn, lead fruitful lives and become truthful witnesses to his legacy of love.

My Sunday Reflection

Who are some of the "prophets" I follow,
and what fruits have their lives borne?

MONDAY

> The tree that is beside the running water is fresher and gives more fruit.
>
> ST. TERESA OF ÁVILA

Where is Jesus planting me? What kind of fruit am I bearing for him?

TUESDAY

> To surround anything, however monstrous or ridiculous, with an air of mystery, is to invest it with a secret charm, and power of attraction which to the crowd is irresistible.
>
> CHARLES DICKENS, *BARNABY RUDGE*

Who have I followed in the past that led me away from Jesus? Why did I choose to follow them?

WEDNESDAY

> My prayers, my God, flow from what I am not;
> I think thy answers make me what I am.
>
> GEORGE MACDONALD, *DIARY OF AN OLD SOUL*

How are my prayer conversations with Jesus inviting me to better understand the person I truly am?

THURSDAY

> God makes all things good; man meddles with them and they become evil.

JEAN-JACQUES ROUSSEAU, *EMILE*

What is a straightforward blessing from Jesus that was tainted by my humanity or someone else's?

FRIDAY

> Life's like a movie, write your own ending
> Keep believing, keep pretending.
> We've done just what we've set out to do
> thanks to the lovers, the dreamers, and you.

THE MUPPET MOVIE, "RAINBOW CONNECTION"

What type of witness do I wish to bear, and how will it lead others to know Jesus?

SATURDAY

> My hand will be against the prophets who see false visions and utter lying divinations; they shall not be in the council of my people, nor be enrolled in the register of the house of Israel, nor shall they enter the land of Israel; and you shall know that I am the LORD GOD.

EZEKIEL 13:9

How can I protect myself from giving trust to false prophets?

Let us pray.

Jesus, you warn me against placing my trust in false prophets.

Instill a spirit of wise discernment that I might knowingly follow those who will lead me closer to you.

As I always strive to be someone who speaks your truths, may the fruits of what you have taught me bless anyone who encounters me.

Let my life forever point to your love.

Amen.

WEEK 26

SUNDAY

Battling Sin with Love

Temptations to Sin—Mark 9:42–50

If your hand causes you to stumble, cut it off; it is better for you to enter life maimed than to have two hands and to go to hell, to the unquenchable fire.

MARK 9:43

IN CAPERNAUM, JESUS WARNED HIS DISCIPLES against temptations to sin. Chastising them against leading others astray, he advised them to examine those parts of themselves that led to sinful behavior. These pathways should be eliminated for the sake of their salvation.

On Saturday mornings when I was growing up, our parents permitted us to watch cartoons for a few hours. I recall a common trope where a character's "shoulder devil" would argue with his "shoulder angel," leading the malleable soul into grave temptation. Typically, but not always, the good guys would win in the end.

The plot device, common in many cultures and faiths, dates back centuries. In many animated versions, the angel and devil are caricature forms of the main character. While it's true that some of us have people in our lives who are bad influences, we can often be our own worst enemies. But before teaching his followers how to eradicate their sources of sin, Jesus warned them against being stumbling blocks for others. When we fail and sin, we don't only hurt ourselves.

Our natures and appetites are unique to each of us. What might be perfectly fine for someone else might be a *No* I need to say to myself. I am constantly working on overcoming the sins that separate me from Jesus. Sin can come in the form of substances, but it can also be attitudinal. Depending upon the day, I might fall prey to all seven deadly sins: pride, greed, lust, envy, gluttony, wrath, and sloth. Eliminating sources of weakness and temptation is a daily or even hourly choice. And it is never easy. Battling sin means facing it head-on, asking for help from Jesus and others, and choosing the best path toward wholeness.

Just as Jesus called his followers to journey together, he invites us to live in community. If we struggle repeatedly with sin, we can seek absolution and healing through the Sacrament of Reconciliation. We may also need the company and encouragement of others who have walked this way before us in support and self-help groups, spiritual direction, therapeutic counseling, and medical interventions. Wholeness begins with one affirmative step toward loving ourselves as much as Jesus loves us.

My Sunday Reflection

What sins or sources of temptation are separating me from Jesus's love?

MONDAY

> Left to our own desires, we make a mess of our lives. But our Creator has shown us the way to true life. To receive the gift of this way is to follow it. This is not a rule for some part of our life called "spiritual." It is a rule for all of life.

JONATHAN WILSON-HARTGROVE,
THE RULE OF SAINT BENEDICT: A CONTEMPORARY PARAPHRASE

How am I creating a rule of life that calls on Jesus when I strive to overcome sin?

TUESDAY

> We are in a battle. There is a fight of faith to be waged. But the way of faith itself is in tune with what God has done and is doing. The road we travel is the well-traveled road of discipleship.

EUGENE H. PETERSON, *A LONG OBEDIENCE IN THE SAME DIRECTION*

When have I felt defeated or powerless? Did I invite Jesus into that moment? What happened?

WEDNESDAY

> Though tempest-toss'd and half a wreck,
> My Saviour thro' the floods I seek;
> Let neither winds nor stormy main,
> Force back my shatter'd bark again.

WILLIAM COWPER, "TEMPTATION"

Why do I sometimes hesitate to expressly ask Jesus for his help in my moments of sin?

THURSDAY

Pain is weakness leaving the body.

UNITED STATES MARINE CORPS

How has acknowledging my sinful nature drawn me closer to Jesus?

FRIDAY

"Now, you see, the world is full of temptations."
"Temptations?"
"Yep, temptations. They're the wrong things that seem right at the time."

PINOCCHIO

What sins most test me? What is Jesus asking me to strip away?

SATURDAY

Because he himself was tested by what he suffered, he is able to help those who are being tested.

HEBREWS 2:18

How might recognizing Jesus's humanity help me grow in my courage and conviction?

Let us pray.

Jesus, you call me to live a life of wholeness and love.

Yet in my weakness, I often choose the path that leads me away from you and others.

Be with me in my brokenness, Lord.

Accompany me as I choose you over sin.

Love me into the newness of life in you.

Amen.

SUNDAY

A Childlike Faith

Jesus Blesses the Children—Luke 18:15–17

But Jesus called for them and said, "Let the little children come to me, and do not stop them; for it is to such as these that the kingdom of God belongs. Truly I tell you, whoever does not receive the kingdom of God as a little child will never enter it."

LUKE 18:16–17

JESUS TOLD HIS FOLLOWERS TWO PARABLES with messages about prayer and humility. The crowds brought their small children to him to beg for his touch upon them. When the disciples tried to block this from happening, Jesus reproached them. He welcomed the children, saying that the kingdom of God truly belongs to them.

I love being in the company of children. As a mother, grandmother, devoted auntie, and children's author, I've come to know and love little ones. I typically seek out the "kids' table" at social gatherings and often intentionally choose the companionship of children over adults.

Our children are born with a childlike dependency that makes them reliant on us for sustenance, shelter, and lessons in socialization. I believe this is part of what Jesus asks of us when reminding us to receive the kingdom of God as children. Our salvation and Jesus's unconditional love are offered with no strings attached. Like a newborn who is offered milk, we are invited to receive Jesus's promises without the expectation of repayment.

But I've also noticed that as our children grow in independence and maturity, they begin to question everything. Any mother will tell you that the *Why* questions that pepper family conversations mark the beginning of a child stepping out into their independent future. As an author, my visits to elementary school classrooms have taught me that young readers have curious minds and discerning tastes. Children rarely filter their commentary and opinions. I endeavor to hear them and not to respond defensively. A child's honest review of my work gives me the best opportunity to learn and grow. I admire their straightforwardness and probing nature.

Receiving the kingdom of heaven as a child does not mean blindly believing. Walking through life alongside little ones has taught me to be generous with signs of affection, to accept gifts with gratitude, but never to stop asking *Why*. Just as we regale our children with stories that have lasting moral values, Jesus speaks to us in parables that help us step closer to the way he desires that we live and love.

Need a lesson in childlike trust? Don't worry. There's always room at the kids' table.

My Sunday Reflection

In what ways am I childlike in my belief?

MONDAY

> God has written a unique and unrepeatable story for each of us, but he lets us write the ending.
>
> ST. CARLO ACUTIS

What plotlines in the story of my life draw me closer to Jesus?

TUESDAY

> A faith that just accepts is a child's faith and all right for children, but eventually you have to grow religiously as every other way, though some never do.
>
> FLANNERY O'CONNOR, *THE HABIT OF BEING*

How does my asking *Why* help me to better know and love Jesus?

WEDNESDAY

> Go out into the darkness and put your hand into the
> Hand of God.
> That shall be to you better than light and safer than
> a known way.
>
> MINNIE LOUISE HASKINS, "THE GATE OF THE YEAR"

When was a time when I trusted Jesus implicitly? What happened?

THURSDAY

> As for Mary, she was little more than a child when the angel came to her; she had not lost her child's creative acceptance of the realities moving on the other side of the everyday world. We lose our ability to see angels as we grow older, and that is a tragic loss.
>
> MADELEINE L'ENGLE, *WALKING ON WATER*

What steps might I take to grow more trusting of Jesus?

FRIDAY

> Everybody, laughing. Then whatever scares you will go away.
>
> *MY NEIGHBOR TOTORO*

How is growing in simplicity a path toward being more like Jesus?

SATURDAY

> Like newborn infants, long for the pure, spiritual milk, so that by it you may grow into salvation—if indeed you have tasted that the Lord is good.
>
> 1 PETER 2:2–3

Why do I struggle with (or readily embrace) childlike belief in Jesus?

Let us pray.

Jesus, you who beckon the littlest among us into the bounty of your love, help me to come into your arms with the trust and humility of a child.

Thank you for understanding my need to ask big questions and to ponder deep thoughts, but also for your word, which calls me ever closer to you.

Amen.

WEEK 28

SUNDAY

The Way to Jesus

Jesus the Way, the Truth, and the Life—John 14:1–14

Jesus said to him, "I am the way, and the truth, and the life. No one comes to the Father except through me. If you know me, you will know my Father also. From now on you do know him and have seen him."

JOHN 14:6–7

ON THE EVENING OF THE LAST SUPPER, after having washed their feet, anticipated Judas's betrayal, and foretold Peter's denial, Jesus encouraged his disciples to have true faith in him. He assured them they would know the way to God. Indeed, by knowing Jesus—God made man—the disciples had all the knowledge they needed to find the way to God. God's house would have ample space for all who knew, trusted, and believed.

I love a good road trip. As a child, I spent countless days journeying with my parents and siblings in our motor home. As an adult, I've enjoyed multiple cross-country adventures. Even with a destination in mind, spontaneous detours thrill me.

Growing up, I loved poring over the Automobile Association maps my parents stocked for our trips. Daddy knew the route to my parents' hometown of Fort Wayne, Indiana, by the landmarks. He never needed a map. But I remember sitting beside him with the map, anticipating the places we would pass.

As a young adult living and working in Los Angeles, I learned to navigate around Southern California with a bulky atlas called *The Thomas Guide*, which held hundreds of pages of gridded maps. I had to flip between grids with one hand and steer with the other. My guardian angel protected me from collisions.

Recently, I have become overly reliant on my phone's GPS. I plug in my destination and follow the digital voice with blind trust. If I intentionally decide to take a different turn, my phone scolds me with the notification that it is rerouting, as if questioning my arrogance for not following its instructions.

I've learned that when it comes to the ultimate destination for my life, I should consistently trust the words Jesus spoke to his disciples when he offered them a precise road map. Jesus, the son of God, is the way, the truth, and the life. I believe this and profess my belief, yet I still occasionally reroute. I can blame my detours on laziness, curiosity, or philosophical differences. But too often, my side ventures happen because of a lack of faith. Like Thomas and Philip, I must be led by the hand back to the proper path. There, Jesus awaits me, ready to lead me home.

My Sunday Reflection

In what ways is Jesus my way, my truth, and my life?

MONDAY

> Therefore hold fast to Christ if you wish to be safe. You will not be able to go astray, because he is the way. He who remains with him does not wander in trackless places; he is on the right way.
>
> ST. THOMAS AQUINAS, *EXPOSITION ON JOHN'S GOSPEL*

How have I allowed Jesus to guide my steps?

TUESDAY

> The way of Jesus cannot be imposed or mapped—it requires an active participation in following Jesus as he leads us through sometimes strange and unfamiliar territory, in circumstances that become clear only in the hesitations and questionings, in the pauses and reflections where we engage in prayerful conversation with one another and with him.
>
> EUGENE H. PETERSON, *THE JESUS WAY*

How do I actively choose to follow the way Jesus points me to?

WEDNESDAY

> Come, my Way, my Truth, my Life:
> Such a way as gives us breath;
> Such a truth as ends all strife,
> Such a life as killeth death.
>
> GEORGE HERBERT, "COME, MY WAY"

Which truth has Jesus taught me that helps me find the path to the peace he offers?

THURSDAY

> I am the Way unchangeable; the Truth infallible; the Life everlasting. I am the Way altogether straight, the Truth supreme, the true Life, the blessed Life, the uncreated Life.

THOMAS Á KEMPIS, *IMITATION OF CHRIST*

When was a moment in my life when I invited Jesus to be in the center of my heart?

FRIDAY

> I love you all, and—oh, Auntie Em—there's no place like home!

THE WIZARD OF OZ

What do I dream that being home with Jesus will look like?

SATURDAY

> We know that we are God's children, and that the whole world lies under the power of the evil one. And we know that the Son of God has come and has given us understanding so that we may know him who is true; and we are in him who is true, in his Son Jesus Christ. He is the true God and eternal life.

1 JOHN 5:19–20

How is Jesus opening my eyes and heart to the truth he teaches?

Let us pray.

Jesus, Son of God and Word made flesh, you are the way, the truth, and the life.

I profess my faith in you with my mouth, but too often my actions lead me astray.

Take my hand, Lord.

Forgive my disbelief when I intentionally venture from the path I know to be right and true.

Lead me home.

Amen.

WEEK 29

SUNDAY

Hope When Life Is Hard

Jesus Thanks His Father—Matthew 11:25–30

Come to me, all you that are weary and are carrying heavy burdens, and I will give you rest. Take my yoke upon you, and learn from me; for I am gentle and humble in heart, and you will find rest for your souls. For my yoke is easy, and my burden is light.

MATTHEW 11:28–30

JESUS OFFERED GRATITUDE TO GOD, calling him Father. He made it clear that he and the Father were one. His mission was divine. Consoling the crowd, he invited those who carried burdens to rest in his care.

Someone I respect very much recently complimented me on my calm nature. "I sense that you are at peace," he said kindly. I held back a laugh and simply thanked him. But his comment stayed with me, and I took it to prayer. The truth, I discovered, was that, for the first time in ages, I did feel an abiding sense of peace. I hadn't even realized it.

Like so many others, my recent life has been filled with stressors. During and immediately following the pandemic, both of my parents experienced health crises and passed away. My grief often felt insurmountable, hitting me in waves of intensity with no rhyme or reason. A year after their funerals, I was diagnosed with breast cancer and went through treatment that left me physically weak and questioning my life's purpose. Looking back now, I recognize that those years felt like a very long, dark tunnel with no light at its end.

During those times when I felt too emotionally and spiritually defeated to pray, I tried to console myself with two fundamental truths: Jesus loves me even in my brokenness, and I do not walk my journey alone. Just as he did for the crowds who gathered around him, Jesus welcomes me into the fullness of his embrace. I have learned to stop chastising myself when my prayer life falls short. Jesus doesn't keep track. I am learning to rest, sure in the knowledge that he loves me just as I am.

Emerging from that dark tunnel has been a gift. But I actually do try to revisit my time of desolation with gratitude. I am surrounded with love. My health is improving. My parents rest in God's embrace, and their suffering is ended forever.

Remembering the darkness prompts me to thank Jesus unceasingly for the good and bad times. It equips me to help people who face their own dark nights of the soul and reminds me that when I experience future trials, as I surely will, hope awaits.

My Sunday Reflection

When I am overburdened, how does Jesus help me find hope?

MONDAY

> Live in faith and hope, though it be in darkness, for in this darkness God protects the soul. Cast your care upon God for you are His and He will not forget you. Do not think that He is leaving you alone, for that would be to wrong Him.
>
> ST. JOHN OF THE CROSS

When did I emerge from a time of darkness, aware of Jesus's nearness and love?

TUESDAY

> The wind came back with triple fury, and put out the light for the last time. . . . They seemed to be staring at the dark, but their eyes were watching God.
>
> ZORA NEALE HURSTON, *THEIR EYES WERE WATCHING GOD*

How might keeping my eyes fixed on Jesus in times of hardship help me feel stronger?

WEDNESDAY

> Hold fast to dreams
> For if dreams die
> Life is a broken-winged bird
> That cannot fly.
>
> LANGSTON HUGHES, "DREAMS"

How might I invite Jesus into moments of despair to find hope?

THURSDAY

> The command of Jesus is hard, unutterably hard, for those who try to resist it. But for those who willingly submit, the yoke is easy, and the burden is light.
>
> DIETRICH BONHOEFFER, *THE COST OF DISCIPLESHIP*

Why am I sometimes unwilling to submit to Jesus's teachings and companionship?

FRIDAY

> And I've learned life is a lot like surfing. When you get caught in the impact zone, you need to get right back up. Because you never know what's over the next wave. And if you have faith, anything is possible, anything at all.
>
> *SOUL SURFER*

How does my faith in Jesus help me to get back up when I've fallen or feel defeated by life?

SATURDAY

> Do not fear, for I am with you,
> do not be dismayed, for I am your God;
> I will strengthen you, I will help you,
> I will uphold you with my victorious right hand.
>
> ISAIAH 41:10

When have I thanked Jesus for being my strength when I feel weak?

Let us pray.

Jesus, gentle and humble of heart, I often come to you with full arms and a heavy heart.

Thank you for helping me bear my burdens.

Open my spirit so I never shy away from the pain others experience.

Use me, even in my brokenness, to help your people know the peace and consolation of your embrace.

Amen.

WEEK 30

SUNDAY

Serving Others with Humility

The Request of James and John—Mark 10:35–45

But it is not so among you; but whoever who wishes to become great among you must be your servant, and whoever wishes to be first among you must be slave of all. For the Son of man came not to be served but to serve, and to give his life as a ransom for many.

MARK 10:43–45

AS THEY WALKED, the brothers James and John approached Jesus and told him they wanted him to comply with their request. The "sons of thunder" were straightforward: "Grant us to sit, one at your right hand and one at your left, in your glory." When Jesus asked them if they were prepared to suffer his same fate, they assured him affirmatively. The remaining ten disciples became indignant. Ultimately, Jesus reminded all of them that he had come to serve, not to be served. Their calling was the same. Whoever of them desired to be the greatest must make it his goal to be the slave to all instead.

My first "real" job out of college was a minimum-wage file clerk role in the personnel office at Vanderbilt University, where Greg attended medical school. It seems my undergraduate French major didn't qualify me for much. However, the personnel manager liked my attitude and seemed confident in my alphabetization skills, so the job was mine. Back in those pre-computer days, my sole responsibility was to wrangle the stacks of paper files that covered my desk all day, every day.

The work was a slog. Brimming with self-confidence, I interiorly lamented that I was underutilized. I left the office every Friday with a file-free desktop, but one of the recruiters worked overtime every weekend. When I returned each Monday, my workspace overflowed with files, and my temper burned.

Over time, I worked my way up through the office. By the time Greg graduated from medical school, I was serving as the manager. I tried my best to treat my fellow staff members with dignity, seeing

and serving Jesus through my work alongside them. I gave extra love to the overburdened file clerks who successively filled my role. Every Monday morning, arriving an hour or two before our doors opened, I prayerfully hustled, clearing away the stacks of weekend files. Doing this in secret became one of my favorite parts of the week. That weekly ritual of putting myself in our clerks' shoes helped me understand the managerial concept of "servant leadership" more than any grad-school course I ever took.

My Sunday Reflection

When did I last serve humbly instead of seeking glory?

MONDAY

I have never felt I am a slave to any man or woman but I am a servant of the Almighty God who made us all. When one of His children is in need, I am glad to be His slave.

VENERABLE PIERRE TOUSSAINT

How did I feel when I intentionally accepted a role in menial service?

TUESDAY

The law of service. He who wishes to live long must serve, but he who wishes to rule does not live long.

HERMANN HESSE, *JOURNEY TO THE EAST*

Who are the service mentors in my life? What have they taught me?

WEDNESDAY

In which class are you? Are you easing the load,
Of overtaxed lifters, who toil down the road?
Or are you a leaner, who lets others share
Your portion of labor, and worry and care?

ELLA WHEELER WILCOX, "THE TWO KINDS OF PEOPLE"

What is an example of a time when I humbly let someone serve me even though it took me out of my comfort zone?

THURSDAY

> The servant-leader is servant first, it begins with a natural feeling that one wants to serve, to serve first, as opposed to wanting power, influence, fame, or wealth.
>
> ROBERT K. GREENLEAF, *SERVANT LEADERSHIP*

How would I describe being a "servant leader" to a friend or coworker?

FRIDAY

> A grown-up would want to do everything his own way, not mine. So that's why I decided a long time ago that I had to find a child.
>
> *WILLY WONKA AND THE CHOCOLATE FACTORY*

Why are children and younger people often able to teach me about serving with joy and humility?

SATURDAY

> My child, perform your tasks
> with humility;
> then you will be loved by those
> whom God accepts.
>
> SIRACH 3:17

What is Jesus asking me to do with love that is hard for me? How will I grow from performing this act of service quietly?

Let us pray.

Jesus, you taught your disciples by example that true leaders put the needs of others before their own glory and recognition.

You call me to serve humbly, quietly, and with great love.

Help me keep my ego intact and see the unspoken wishes of those around me.

I feel blessed to call myself a slave for your love.

Amen.

WEEK 31

SUNDAY

Straining to Be with Jesus

Jesus and Zacchaeus—Luke 19:1–10

He was trying to see who Jesus was, but on account of the crowd he could not, because he was short in stature. So he ran ahead and climbed a sycamore tree to see him, because he was going to pass that way.

LUKE 19:3–4

AS JESUS ENTERED JERICHO, the chief tax collector, Zacchaeus, was anxious to see him. He climbed a tree because he was too short to have a vantage point amid the crowds. Jesus spotted him and asked him to host dinner. Amid grumbles that Jesus was dining with a sinner, Zacchaeus repented and was saved.

I can relate to Zacchaeus's creative solution to fulfill his desire to get close to Jesus. Several times in my life, I've found myself in large crowds. There is always a sense of anticipation and a grave FOMO (fear of missing out).

If we aren't wealthy enough to pay for the VIP seats at a music festival, we arrive early to have a shot at standing near the stage, if only for a few moments. As a Disney enthusiast, I enjoy spending days and evenings with friends at the parks. It's normal to see parents along the parade routes elevating their little ones to sit atop their shoulders for a closer glance at their favorite characters. At baseball games, we watch warm-ups, hoping our favorite player might stop by for an autograph or toss us a ball.

What would I do if I heard that Jesus was coming to my town? Like Zacchaeus, I'd be seeking the best view. I might strategize how to ask for a selfie to share on social media. I would video the encounter to rewatch later with my friends. If he came close enough, I might hand Jesus an autographed copy of one of my books. I would be nervous, excited, and filled with hopeful anticipation. And if Jesus went as far as to invite himself over for dinner, I would probably worry about what food I had on hand or how messy my home looked.

I miss too many chances to encounter the living Jesus. After receiving the Eucharist, I often neglect to fall to my knees in wonder at his nearness in the true presence. Jesus is around me all day, every day, in the people I meet, the divinity of natural creation, and the love surrounding me. It's time to eagerly welcome him, just as I am, into the home of my heart.

My Sunday Reflection

How am I willing to strive to see and encounter Jesus daily?

MONDAY

> How many of you say: I should like to see His face, His garments, His shoes. You do see Him, you touch Him, you eat Him. He gives Himself to you, not only that you may see Him, but also to be your food and nourishment.
>
> ST. JOHN CHRYSOSTOM

How do I express my longing to see and be with Jesus?

TUESDAY

> What are you in love with? What fascinates you? What intrigues you and captures your imagination? Nothing will affect your life more than whom and what you choose to love.
>
> MATTHEW KELLY, *THE SEVEN LEVELS OF INTIMACY*

Why am I choosing to pursue my love for Jesus at this time in my life?

WEDNESDAY

> I'd rather learn from one bird how to sing
> than teach ten thousand stars how not to dance
>
> E. E. CUMMINGS,
> "YOU SHALL ABOVE ALL THINGS BE GLAD AND YOUNG"

Where have I encountered Jesus and missed his presence? What might I have learned if I'd been more attuned to him?

THURSDAY

> You—with all your weaknesses and flaws—were made for this. You—in all of your struggles and pain—are enough.
>
> DANIELLE BEAN, *YOU ARE ENOUGH*

What reminds me that I am worthy of an encounter with Jesus?

FRIDAY

> I came here tonight because when you realize you want to spend the rest of your life with somebody, you want the rest of your life to start as soon as possible.
>
> *WHEN HARRY MET SALLY*

How will meeting Jesus begin my life anew?

SATURDAY

> "Come," my heart says, "seek his face!"
> Your face, LORD, do I seek.
> Do not hide your face from me.
>
> PSALM 27:8–9

Where have I sought and found Jesus?

Let us pray.

Jesus, you sought out Zacchaeus and offered him the encounter of a lifetime.

In return, he gave you his heart and life.

I long to see you, Lord.

Yet too often I miss your nearness in my busyness and distraction.

Come into my being and dwell within me.

In your loving presence, I am forever found.

Amen.

WEEK 32

SUNDAY

Bearing Fruit

Jesus the True Vine—John 15:1–17

Abide in me as I abide in you. Just as the branch cannot bear fruit by itself unless it abides in the vine, neither can you unless you abide in me. I am the vine, you are the branches. Those who abide in me and I in them bear much fruit, because apart from me you can do nothing.

JOHN 15:4–5

WHILE GATHERING WITH HIS DISCIPLES over supper, Jesus spoke about his greatest commandment: that they love one another. He used the example of a vineyard, calling himself the vine and his Father the vine grower. He summoned his friends to bear great fruit by their lives but reminded them that this could happen only if they remained in close, loving relationship with him and with one another. This is the closeness that still binds us together as a community.

We raised our sons in California's Central Valley, near an area called "the raisin capital of the world." As kindergarteners, both boys began their school years with a lesson on raisin cultivation since the region was home to many farmers. We learned that the process of growing raisins is complicated. Despite technological advances, some aspects of propagation have remained consistent for centuries. This includes the final stage of the process, when clusters of grapes are laid on paper "trays" in east-to-west rows where the sun naturally dries the crops. Left to bake for two to three weeks, the raisins, which have already withstood pruning, potential pest infestation, and drought, can be ruined by one last threat. An abundance of rain can devastate an entire year's crop. When I see a vineyard, I think of wine varietals, but I also remember the complexities of growing the humble raisin.

As followers of Jesus, we are not all that different from those raisins that flourish in the California sunshine. Left to our own devices, we face many challenges. Our world is filled with crop-ruining potential. Just as a raisin cannot be adequately raised when a step of the process is neglected, much goes into ensuring that we remain tightly bonded to all that Jesus desires for our lives.

Thankfully, we are never left to grow on our own. Jesus's words in Scripture prune us. We find room to grow in the warmth and security of his love. By surrounding ourselves with good friends and loved ones, we are less likely to be victimized by pests. Our crop flourishes when we love one another and remain unafraid to lay down our lives for our friends. Nurtured with care, the fruit of our lives is diverse, prolific, and incredibly sweet.

My Sunday Reflection

How does the love of Jesus and others help me to bear fruit?

MONDAY

> The fruit of silence is prayer. The fruit of prayer is faith. The fruit of faith is love. The fruit of love is service. The fruit of service is peace.

MOTHER TERESA, *A SIMPLE PATH*

What is the fruit of my relationship with Jesus?

TUESDAY

> The outer action of respect is born from the inner quality of reverence, and that reverence is the fruit of reflection, which helps us to see people and things in their true value.

MATTHEW KELLY, *THE SEVEN LEVELS OF INTIMACY*

Why is being in right relationships with others crucial to my love for Jesus?

WEDNESDAY

> I'm only a fragile Branch,
> I live by a life not mine,
> For the sap that flows through my tendrils small
> Is the life-blood of the Vine.

FREDA HANBURY ALLEN, "A BRANCH"

When has Jesus used me to help someone?

THURSDAY

> And for my part, I shall not wholly fail of my task, though Gondor should perish, if anything passes through this night that can still grow fair or bear fruit and flower again in days to come. For I also am a steward.

J. R. R. TOLKIEN, *THE RETURN OF THE KING*

How am I acting as a steward of the love Jesus has planted in me?

FRIDAY

> To love another person is to see the face of God.

LES MISÉRABLES

In what ways am I trying to lay down my life for those I love?

SATURDAY

> She rises while it is still night
> and provides food for her household
> and tasks for her servant-girls.
> She considers a field and buys it;
> with the fruit of her hands she plants a vineyard.

PROVERBS 31:15–16

How would I describe the vineyard of my life? Is Jesus present there?

Let us pray.

Jesus, true vine, you call me into a relationship of growth.

Plant the seeds of your will deep in my soul.

Nourish them with your word and your presence, made manifest in the Eucharist.

Surround me with others so that I may practice the self-giving love you desire to perfect in me.

The humble fruit of my life is yours.

Amen.

WEEK 33

SUNDAY

Sowing Seeds of Hope

The Parable of the Sower—Matthew 13:1–9

Other seeds fell on good soil and brought forth grain, some a hundredfold, some sixty, some thirty. Let anyone with ears listen!

MATTHEW 13:8–9

THEY CROWDED AROUND JESUS along the shore of the Sea of Galilee, eager for his wisdom. He taught them from a boat on the lake, his words amplifying across the water. Their hearts stirred with the word pictures he painted, carrying them to a path littered with seeds too quickly snatched away by hungry crows. Next, they imagined scorched terrain, entirely unwelcoming for new life. This gave way to a thorny scrub where the seeds they mentally sowed were choked away to nothingness. Finally, the crowd pictured verdant soil where the seeds they sowed grew into basketfuls of nourishing grain.

I gathered with friends one early June weekend to celebrate Cancer Survivor Day. The event's organizers told us that we became "survivors" the day we were diagnosed and took a single, hopeful step toward healing. At the celebration, we painted simple terra cotta pots, filled them with loamy soil, and sowed packets of wildflower seeds in the small clay vessels.

That afternoon, I christened my pot of dirt with the name "Hope." Five days later, when I embarked on a summer road trip, I tucked Hope into the cupholder of my car and set out to visit family and friends. That first driving day, Hope's pot contained a single tiny green shoot, just large enough to convince me that if I tended my plant carefully, it might one day hold the promise of a flower.

Hope the plant accompanied me as I covered more than seven thousand miles and spent six blessed weeks in the company of loved ones. Many mornings, new shoots sprouted amid others that were already flourishing. Upon my return home, I replanted Hope's scores of tiny seedlings in my garden.

The fields of our lives are often filled with the hungriness of distraction, the scorched soil of despair, or the thorns of anxiety. Caring for Hope's blossoms taught me that the potential for the incredible good that God wants for us is often invisible—until it isn't. Christ's love and goodness flourish when we intentionally sow the seeds of our lives and tend to them with love, trust, and hope.

My Sunday Reflection

How has experiencing the growth of something or someone helped me to have hope in my life?

MONDAY

> Consult not your fears but your hopes and your dreams. Think not about your frustrations, but about your unfulfilled potential. Concern yourself not with what you tried and failed in, but with what it is still possible for you to do.
>
> ST. JOHN XXIII

What is still possible in my life? How does having trust in Jesus drive me toward this hope?

TUESDAY

> Create no images of God. Accept the images that God has provided. They are everywhere, in everything. God is Change—Seed to tree, tree to forest; Rain to river, river to sea; Grubs to bees, bees to swarm. From one, many; from many, one; Forever uniting, growing, dissolving—forever Changing. The universe is God's self-portrait.
>
> OCTAVIA E. BUTLER, *PARABLE OF THE SOWER*

Where in natural imagery have I recognized the face of Jesus lately? How did spotting seeds of the divine make me feel?

WEDNESDAY

> How Love burns through the Putting in the Seed
> On through the watching for that early birth.
>
> ROBERT FROST, "PUTTING IN THE SEED"

What seed has Jesus asked me to plant that is still dormant? How will I greet its birth and nurture it?

THURSDAY

> I've never doubted my faith. But did I have courage? Did I trust Jesus? Ah. That's the slow-growing bloom of faith. Faith is the seed. But courage and trust? That's later. That's a result. It's the result of a lot of dark nights and lots of tears and feelings of *this is never going to happen*.
>
> EMILY DEARDO, AUTHOR OF *LIVING MEMENTO MORI*

What is the fruit of the seeds that I have planted? How can I tend to them so that they will bear the fruit of Jesus's love in others?

FRIDAY

> Legacy. What is a legacy? It's planting seeds in a garden you never get to see.
>
> LIN-MANUEL MIRANDA, "THE WORLD WAS WIDE ENOUGH,"
> *HAMILTON: AN AMERICAN MUSICAL*

How would I describe the garden of my life? What seeds are blooming in me? Who did Jesus send to plant those seeds in me?

SATURDAY

> Sow for yourselves righteousness:
> reap steadfast love;
> break up your fallow ground;
> for it is the time to seek the LORD,
> that he may come and rain righteousness upon you.
>
> HOSEA 10:12

Where will I seek Jesus today? How might he unexpectedly rain salvation into my life?

Let us pray.

Jesus, master gardener, your love has borne a bountiful harvest in my life.

Make of my heart a fertile field, fully receptive to the seeds of your love.

Help me to clear away the weeds and thorns that choke your will for me.

Plant generatively in me, Lord, so that others may discover your seeds and bloom with hope.

Amen.

SUNDAY

Cleansing Our Temples

Jesus Cleanses the Temple—Mark 11:15–19

Then they came to Jerusalem. And he entered the temple and began to drive out those who were selling and those who were buying in the temple, and he overturned the tables of the money changers and the seats of those who sold doves; and he would not allow anyone to carry anything through the temple.

MARK 11:15–16

JESUS MADE HIS TRIUMPHAL ENTRY into Jerusalem. Riding on the back of a donkey colt, he was greeted with cries of "Hosanna!" The next day, he cursed a fruit tree that had neglected to bear fruit. He entered the temple and began acting against the many money changers and merchants using that holy place for ill-gotten gains. Jesus's actions were a cleansing and a transformation of the temple, a symbol of hope for all. The chief priests and scribes feared the impact he had on those who gathered to hear his teachings.

As children, my siblings and I learned from the Franciscan sisters who educated us that our bodies were "temples of the Holy Spirit." We were taught to keep our bodies chaste and pure since God dwelled within us. That concept didn't make much sense to me back then, when my worst offenses involved sneaking candy before dinner or breaking a fast before Mass.

Now I understand much more clearly what the sisters were saying. I am made in God's image and likeness. The true presence of Jesus—body, blood, soul, and divinity—dwells in me whenever I receive the Eucharist. When I really stop and ponder this, I lament the dirty state of my bodily vessel as a receptacle for God's love. But I find comfort in my wholehearted trust in Jesus's mercy, even in my unworthiness.

I often hear cries from the heart and loud objections from friends and family who have made conscious decisions to step away from the practice of organized religion. Their reasons are varied, and their hurt feels insurmountable. For them, as the only person they know who is still practicing, I often represent "church." They come to me to argue, weep, make jokes, or ask big, challenging questions. If I am a hypocrite, their trust in me and in Jesus's church is battered.

I am learning to listen more and to speak less. What my loved ones usually need from me in their moments of vulnerability, honesty, hurt, or anger is not a homily or a word of apologetics. It's not my job to talk them into anything. Instead, Jesus asks me to be a living temple of his love that meets and welcomes people wherever they may be on their spiritual journey. This means having that pure, trusting heart the Franciscan sisters taught me to cultivate. When I cleanse my personal temple, Jesus can and will work in whatever way that best comforts those who most need to know his love.

My Sunday Reflection

How might I cleanse my temple as a messenger of Jesus's unfailing love?

MONDAY

> Those whose hearts are pure are temples of the Holy Spirit.

ST. LUCY

How might I seek a pure heart that is more like Jesus's?

TUESDAY

> Jesus overturned money-changing tables in the temple, but set up banqueting tables in his Father's house.

BRIAN ZAHND, *WATER TO WINE*

When am I a part of the communion Jesus desires in our broken world?

WEDNESDAY

> This my vile body Thou dost take,
> And thinkest fit
> To honour it,
> And for Thy use a house it make.

THOMAS WASHBOURNE, "THE TEMPLE OF THE HOLY GHOST"

Where am I making changes to more lovingly welcome Jesus to dwell in me?

THURSDAY

> Please cleanse me, even if I must endure hardship or suffer affliction in the process. . . . Then let me rejoice when Your temple is again pure.
>
> CHARLES R. SWINDOLL, *LIVING INSIGHTS: JOHN*

Why have I misunderstood Jesus's wrath in the temple? What does it mean to me now?

FRIDAY

> No matter how filthy something gets, you can always clean it right up.
>
> *BRUCE ALMIGHTY*

How can I trust the change that Jesus desires to create in my life?

SATURDAY

> Do you not know that you are God's temple and that God's Spirit dwells in you? If any one destroys God's temple, God will destroy him. For God's temple is holy, and you are that temple.
>
> 1 CORINTHIANS 3:16–17

When have I felt Jesus reaching out to others through his love for me?

Let us pray.

Jesus, bold and beloved, you call me to serve as your living temple.

Dwell within me and light my path with the fire of your love.

Purify me, Lord, so I might have clarity of purpose and a soul worthy of any mission.

Use me wherever you send me to bear fruit in your name.

Hosanna in the highest!

Amen.

WEEK 35

SUNDAY

Faith and the Public Life

The Question about Paying Taxes—Luke 20:20–26

[Jesus said,] "Show me a denarius. Whose head and whose title does it bear?" They said, "The emperor's." He said to them, "Then give to the emperor the things that are the emperor's, and to God the things that are God's."

LUKE 20:24–25

THE SCRIBES AND CHIEF PRIESTS SURVEILLED JESUS and sent spies to entrap him. They asked about the lawfulness of paying taxes to the emperor. Jesus encouraged them all to peaceably follow the laws of the land.

Helping my eldest register for selective service and cast his first ballot when he turned eighteen filled me with joy. I've always cherished my right to vote and did my best to instill this same sense of patriotic duty in my sons. Discussing candidates and issues as a family, and accompanying my young adult sons to the precinct as they cast their ballots was not a duty but a cherished honor and privilege.

When Jesus taught his followers to "give to the emperor," he wasn't simply looking to avoid falling into a political trap his enemies were laying for him. Living as a person of faith means taking a holistic approach toward exercising civic duties. To live as a faithful follower of Jesus means to follow his teachings on caring for our neighbor, seeking peace, respecting authority, and conforming with social structures that promote the common good for humankind. Our faith is not just a belief but a guiding light in our civic responsibilities.

Unfortunately, today's political structure often seems fraught with the potential for uncivilized behavior. Political candidates at almost every level seem to spend more time tearing one another down than proposing solutions that will benefit everyone. But respecting authority requires navigating these battlefields, prayerfully discerning, and participating in the structures that appoint and empower our leaders. In these challenging times, our determination to engage positively becomes even more critical, giving us hope for a better future.

My friend Lisa is one of my mentors in this respect. Deeply concerned for her neighbors, Lisa has found myriad ways to serve on volunteer boards and civic panels in our city. The annual street fair she helped to launch now gathers thousands of families who formerly coexisted anonymously. Rather than simply complain about the issues plaguing us, Lisa models a "How can I help?" attitude that gets things accomplished. Her motivation is not to scale political rankings. It is to serve our neighborhood lovingly. Jesus calls us to live as forces for good, envisioning and moving together toward the change our world greatly needs.

My Sunday Reflection

How does my love for Jesus impact how I live in society?

MONDAY

> Justice is to be observed not merely in the distribution of wealth, but also in regard to the conditions under which [all people] engage in productive activity. There is, in fact, an innate need of human nature requiring that [people] engaged in productive activity have an opportunity to assume responsibility and to perfect themselves by their efforts.

ST. JOHN XXIII, *MATER ET MAGISTRA*

In what ways am I involved in productively supporting my community and my nation?

TUESDAY

> Citizenship is an attitude, a state of mind, an emotional conviction that the whole is greater than the part . . . and that the part should be humbly proud to sacrifice itself that the whole may live.

ROBERT A. HEINLEIN, *STARSHIP TROOPERS*

When have I sacrificed personally for the good of my neighbors?

WEDNESDAY

> Give me your tired, your poor,
> Your huddled masses yearning to breathe free,
> The wretched refuse of your teeming shore.
> Send these, the homeless, tempest-tost to me,
> I lift my lamp beside the golden door!

EMMA LAZARUS, "THE NEW COLOSSUS"

What does Jesus teach me about welcoming and loving those most in need?

THURSDAY

> Each time a man stands up for an ideal, or acts to improve the lot of others, or strikes out against injustice, he sends forth a tiny ripple of hope, and crossing each other from a million different centers of energy and daring those ripples build a current which can sweep down the mightiest walls of oppression and resistance.

ROBERT KENNEDY, "RIPPLE OF HOPE"
UNIVERSITY OF CAPE TOWN, JUNE 6, 1966

As a follower of Jesus, what are some ways I am called to fight injustice?

FRIDAY

> I find it poor logic to say that because women are good, women should vote. Men do not vote because they are good; they vote because they are male, and women should vote, not because we are angels and men are animals, but because we are human beings and citizens of this country.

LITTLE WOMEN (1994 movie)

When have I committed myself to faithful voting or other forms of civic duty?

SATURDAY

> But our citizenship is in heaven, and it is from there that we are expecting a Savior, the Lord Jesus Christ. He will transform the body of our humiliation that it may be conformed to the body of his glory, by the power that also enables him to make all things subject to himself.

PHILIPPIANS 3:20–21

In what ways do I count myself as a citizen of heaven, and how does this impact my participation in social structures?

Let us pray.

Jesus, you taught your followers to respect the leaders of your day peacefully.

Help me to engage in my civic duties with humility and faith.

Bless, protect, and enlighten our leaders, Lord.

When called to serve my neighbors, may I always extend myself and the gifts you have given me with generosity and compassion.

Amen.

WEEK 36

SUNDAY

Places of Peace

Peace for the Disciples—John 16:25–33

The hour is coming, indeed it has come, when you will be scattered, each one to his home, and you will leave me alone. Yet I am not alone, because the Father is with me. I have said this to you, so that in me you may have peace. In the world you face persecution. But take courage; I have overcome the world.

JOHN 16:32–33

JESUS CONTINUED ENCOURAGING HIS DISCIPLES, promising that he would soon speak clearly about his future. He reminded them that God, his Father, loved them and had sent him to be with them. Jesus assured them that although persecution awaited, he had conquered the world and its tribulations.

I have discovered places where I seek refuge and peace when life's trials overwhelm me. My parish church is one of these. Quiet time in the pews brings healing. But I also shelter in places that are less traditionally religious.

These sacred spaces are essential to my peace. Just as Jesus alerted his friends, "In the world you face persecution," you and I are not exempt from spiritual and earthly warfare. I recognize this warfare in its many forms. Some persecution is imposed by others: those who act against me because of my beliefs, out of envy, or from their own brokenness. Some of it I heap on myself: excoriating myself for my vices, intentionally choosing the less healthy path, or succumbing to extreme guilt for my human frailty.

I am still working on quieting my doom spiral when these moments hit. Prayer time reminds me that I do not face my battles alone. Undoubtedly, the Jesus who stood before his disciples only a few days before he would be crucified and proclaimed that he had "conquered the world" was aiming to teach us that the defeats of this world have nothing to do with what awaits us in the next. Jesus redefined what it means to "conquer" the world. Our small *#winning* moments in this life are fleeting. True victory will never be won here on earth.

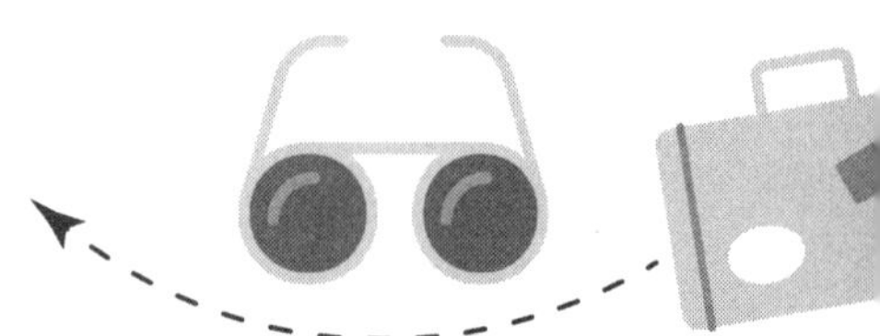

So, when the persecution feels too intense, I find respite in pilgrimages to my places of peace.

I unburden myself honestly to my husband while I rest in the solace of his embrace. I drive in my car blasting music or walk on the beach with the wind blowing in my face to feel the nearness of the Holy Spirit. I hike a nearby trail where the trees whisper God's nearness. Peace is a state of mind and sometimes a destination where Jesus is meant to be found and embraced.

My Sunday Reflection

Where are my places of peace?

MONDAY

> Thou hast made us for thyself, O Lord, and our heart is restless until it finds its rest in thee.
>
> ST. AUGUSTINE OF HIPPO, *CONFESSIONS*

What persecution have I faced? How did I seek peace in that moment?

TUESDAY

> We are invited to look down on this creation with the same perspective as that of the Trinity, looking down at all the plain of the world, and to look up to the rest of the universe as well. Why? Because when we gaze upon the cosmos, we gaze upon the place where we encounter God.
>
> GUY CONSOLMAGNO, SJ, *A JESUIT'S GUIDE TO THE STARS*

How might contemplating the world from Jesus's perspective bring me peace?

WEDNESDAY

> Here is the port of peace and restfulness
> To them that stand in storms and disease,
> Refuge overt to wretches in distress,
> And all comfort from mischief and misease.
>
> JOHN WALTON, "GOD, THE PORT OF PEACE"

When have I found peace and refuge in nature?

THURSDAY

> There is no need to go to India or anywhere else to find peace. You will find that deep place of silence right in your room, your garden or even your bathtub.
>
> ELISABETH KÜBLER-ROSS

Where in my home do I go to encounter the peace of Jesus?

FRIDAY

> God's place is all around us, it is in everything and in anything we can experience. People just need to change the way they look at things.
>
> *INTO THE WILD*

What conflict or disturbance of peace is Jesus inviting me to conquer in my life?

SATURDAY

> I will both lie down and sleep in peace;
> for you alone, O Lord, make me lie down in safety.
>
> PSALM 4:8

Why do I feel at peace knowing that Jesus is always with me?

Let us pray.

Jesus, conqueror of all the world's strife,
thank you for meeting me in my moments of persecution, desolation, and defeat.

Your love is always greater than the worst of my trials.

Meet me where I have been defeated.

Find me when I am lost.

Wrap me in the peace of your true presence.

Amen.

WEEK 37

SUNDAY

Walking on Water

Jesus Walks on the Sea—Matthew 14:22–33

But when the disciples saw him walking on the sea, they were terrified, saying, "It is a ghost!" And they cried out for fear. But immediately Jesus spoke to them and said, "Take heart, it is I; do not be afraid."

MATTHEW 14:26–27

IT HAD BEEN A LONG DAY. Jesus needed time to himself. He ushered the disciples into a boat, dismissed the crowds, and headed to a deserted place to pray. But when a storm kicked up, the disciples became terrified. Seeing someone walking toward them across the sea, they assumed it was a ghost. Jesus immediately revealed himself and beckoned Peter to walk to him with a single word: *Come.* And for one moment of incredible faith, Peter strode atop the waves. But in an instant, he lost trust and began to sink. Jesus was there to save him, but he also chastised Peter for his lack of faith. When the two entered the boat, the wind stopped, and the boatful of followers praised the Lord.

In 2012, I found myself aboard a "Jesus Boat" on the waters of the Sea of Galilee. Approximately thirty-three miles in circumference, the freshwater lake was choppy the day we visited. Gray clouds overhead threatened rain. Even though we voyaged in the daylight, it was easy for me to imagine the fear the disciples might have felt as waves tossed their small craft in pitch black, and a being strode atop the waves toward them.

I have certainly had "Peter moments" in my life. Quick to give myself over to Jesus's will, I jump headlong into whatever mission I perceive my Lord is sending me. I'm quick to give my *Yes* without discernment. But when waves hit me in the face, my trust can be quick to falter. Too often, I rely on "Lisa power," neglecting to invoke the One who invited me out onto the water in the first place. Consolation comes in remembering Jesus's words to his friends, *Take heart, it is I; do not be afraid.*

Our acts of "walking on water" can be big, life-changing moments or simple tests of everyday life. When we doubt and begin to sink, as we most assuredly will, we can always cry out, "Lord, save me," and be ushered into the safety of the boat with Jesus at our side. But let's never allow our fear of sinking to prevent us from walking on water when our Lord invites us to *Come*.

My Sunday Reflection

How is Jesus asking me to walk on water?

MONDAY

> And as when a nestling has come out of the nest before the time, and is on the point of falling, its mother bears it on her wings, and brings it back to the nest; even so did Christ.

ST. JOHN CHRYSOSTOM, *PATRISTIC BIBLE COMMENTARY*, MATTHEW 14:31

How would I describe my trust in Jesus?

TUESDAY

> When we were children, we used to think that when we were grown up we would no longer be vulnerable. But to grow up is to accept vulnerability.

MADELEINE L'ENGLE, *WALKING ON WATER*

How is Jesus asking me to be vulnerable in my self-giving?

WEDNESDAY

> If you can fill the unforgiving minute
> With sixty seconds' worth of distance run,
> Yours is the Earth and everything that's in it,
> And—which is more—you'll be a Man, my son!

RUDYARD KIPLING, "IF"

When has Jesus helped me to be bold? What happened as a result?

THURSDAY

Faith is taking the first step even when you don't see the whole staircase.

MARTIN LUTHER KING JR., CENTENNIAL ANNIVERSARY OF THE PRELIMINARY EMANCIPATION PROCLAMATION

What does stepping out in faith look like for me today?

FRIDAY

Dear child, be brave no matter how hopeless it all seems.

THE BLACK CAT (1934 movie)

How does my faith in Jesus help me to be brave in the face of challenges?

SATURDAY

Be strong and bold; have no fear or dread of them, because it is the LORD your God who goes with you; he will not fail you or forsake you.

DEUTERONOMY 31:6

What do I fear? How does inviting Jesus to walk with me ease my fears?

Let us pray.

Jesus, you extend your hand and ask me to *Come* into places that are sometimes lonely or frightening.

I want to walk toward you, but sometimes I lack faith.

Help me to set aside my fears and believe in the goodness of your will for my life, even when the way forward is obscure and perilous.

I trust that you will never leave me alone.

Amen.

WEEK 38

SUNDAY

Loving and Listening

The First Commandment—Mark 12:28–34

Jesus answered, "The first is, 'Hear, O Israel: the Lord our God, the Lord is one; you shall love the Lord your God with all your heart, and with all your soul, and with all your mind, and with all your strength.' The second is this, 'You shall love your neighbor as yourself.' There is no other commandment greater than these."

MARK 12:29–31

HAVING HEARD JESUS QUESTIONED BY PHARISEES, Herodians, and Sadducees, a scribe approached Jesus and asked him what the first commandment was. Jesus spoke the words of an ancient prayer, the Shema, which he would have recited since boyhood. *Hear, O Israel*, he prayed. Jesus taught that along with loving God limitlessly, we should love our neighbors as ourselves.

I recently encountered a religious sister who had spent most of her career serving in social-service agencies. After her lecture on "Blessed Encounters with the Homeless," I queried Sister, sharing that I have struggled mightily with issues related to the disparity of wealth. During her lecture, Sister spoke about encounters with unhoused neighbors and the lessons she learned from each. I walked away from our conversation with some helpful tips. The one that helped me most was Sister's reminder to stop and deeply listen to those we encounter. Her perception was that when her new homeless friends felt heard, they felt as if they had been treated with respect.

Since that enlightening conversation with Sister, I have focused on the connection between loving and listening. I realize that listening to and hearing God are neglected parts of my prayer journey. Shortly after meeting with Sister, I went camping with a friend for three days. Our time in the mountains was a revelation for me. God spoke to me in the trill of the birds in the trees, the wind rustling through the canyon, the crackling of our campfire, and especially the sound of my dear friend's voice. The quiet of our remote camp spot helped me hear and appreciate these divine love letters I'd been missing from God.

This time spent in nature refueled me to reenter a busy season of my life with a reminder of how deeply God loves me. Bolstered in this way, I felt anxious to share the blessings I had received with everyone I met. The most significant difference was my desire to talk less and to listen more intentionally. I now understand that listening is one of the most important ways I'm called to love others.

My Sunday Reflection

How might I strive to increase my listening to Jesus and my neighbors?

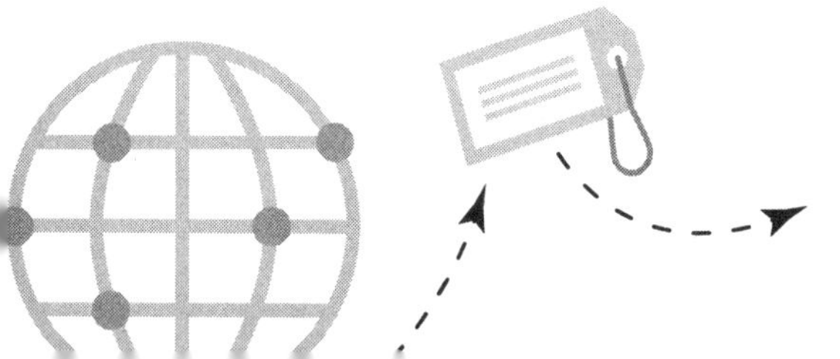

MONDAY

> Listen carefully, my son, to your master's precepts, and incline the ear of your heart.
>
> ST. BENEDICT, *RULE OF ST. BENEDICT*

What prevents me from listening to Jesus in my prayer life?

TUESDAY

> People generally see what they look for, and hear what they listen for.
>
> HARPER LEE, *TO KILL A MOCKINGBIRD*

When did I intentionally listen to a loved one? What did I learn?

WEDNESDAY

> How do I listen to others?
> As if everyone were my Master
> Speaking to me his cherished last words.
>
> HAFIZ, "HOW DO I LISTEN?"

Why do I feel loved when I am heard?

THURSDAY

> In the Church, too, there is a great need to listen to and to hear one another. It is the most precious and life-giving gift we can offer each other.
>
> POPE FRANCIS, "LISTENING WITH THE EAR OF THE HEART," 56TH WORLD DAY OF SOCIAL COMMUNICATIONS

How can I enter an authentic dialogue with my neighbors about Jesus's love?

FRIDAY

> He's like a lot of people around here. He just wants somebody to listen.
>
> *GREMLINS* (1984 movie)

Who is waiting for me to listen to them lovingly?

SATURDAY

> So faith comes from what is heard, and what is heard comes through the word of Christ.
>
> ROMANS 10:17

What are the words Jesus is speaking into my heart this week?

Let us pray.

Jesus, open my ears to hear your voice amid life's tumult and noise.

May my heart and mind be stilled to know the depths of your love for me.

In turn, help me listen to and deeply love my neighbors—those known to me and those you send into my path.

I love you with all my heart, soul, mind, and strength.

Amen.

WEEK 39

SUNDAY

Our Whole Livelihood

The Widow's Offering—Luke 21:1–4

He said, "Truly I tell you, this poor widow has put in more than all of them; for all of them have contributed out of their abundance, but she out of her poverty has put in all she had to live on."

LUKE 21:3–4

IN EARLY 2016, I was selected to be part of a team of journalists who traveled together on a mission to South America. Our fact-finding journey included observing the work of Catholic Relief Service Rice Bowl projects. As part of an annual Lenten giving campaign, families, parishes, and classrooms place their donations—often simple coins—into small cardboard boxes. The funds collected support families experiencing hunger and bleak futures around the world.

One highlight of the trip was visiting a beneficiary of Rice Bowl funds, Maria, whose college scholarship enabled her to study agriculture. When our team arrived at Maria's simple home, with its corrugated tin roof and walls constructed of heavy green tarps, Maria and her family were standing out front to greet us. Maria pointed to a nearby stack of cinder blocks, communicating excitedly that the money she had earned working as a consultant to local coffee farmers had enabled her family to purchase these building supplies. Soon the walls of their home would be fortified with those bricks.

Maria and her mother prepared for us a feast of empanadas, rice, beans, cheese, omelets, and rich hot chocolate. Maria's photo and her story detailing the good news of her scholarship had appeared in Rice Bowl literature that year; over breakfast, the CRS team surprised the family with an updated cardboard Rice Bowl box, now graced with Maria's smiling face.

As a parting gift, fellow traveler Fr. Rafael blessed Maria's family and their home. Amid hugs and heartfelt goodbyes, Maria slipped the little box into the priest's hand. She had penned her family's name on the side, and we heard the jingling of the few coins she

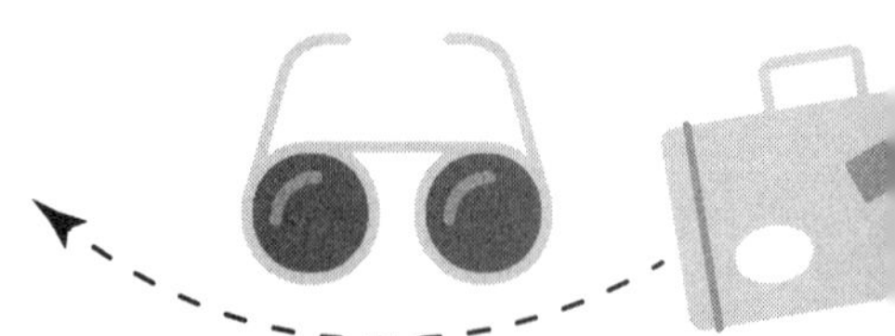

had placed inside. Struggling to choke back tears, Fr. Rafael was still grappling with the grace of this moment when Maria's father and brother stepped forward to add their own humble offerings. Father shared that during his priesthood, he had preached scores of homilies on the parable of the widow's mite (Luke 21:1–4), but we all agreed that our understanding of the Gospel parable was forever changed. Even now, when I read this passage of Luke's Gospel, my heart travels across the miles to Maria, who taught me what giving out of one's poverty truly means.

My Sunday Reflection

What am I willing to give to Jesus today?

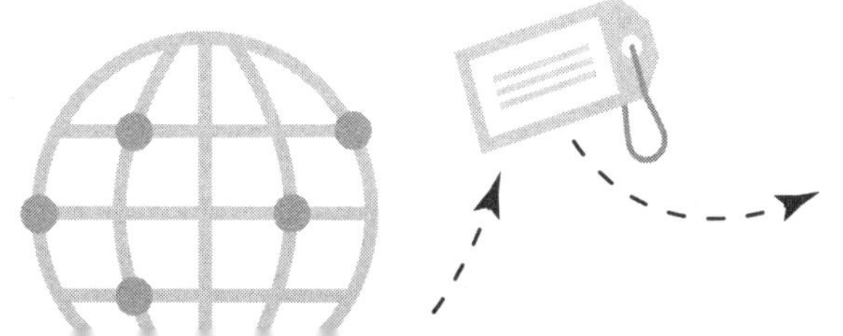

MONDAY

> Give something, however small, to the one in need. For it is not small to one who has nothing. Neither is it small to God, if we have given what we could.
>
> ST. GREGORY NAZIANZEN

What is one small gift I can share today with someone in physical, emotional, or spiritual need?

TUESDAY

> If the logic of worldliness is the drive to get on and go up—to grasp, to absorb, to gain, to conquer—the logic of the incarnation and the reign of God announced by Jesus goes in the opposite direction.
>
> AUSTEN IVEREIGH,
> *FIRST BELONG TO GOD: ON RETREAT WITH POPE FRANCIS*

What is my attitude toward sharing my gifts with others? How does trying to be less worldly help me feel closer to Jesus?

WEDNESDAY

> What can I give Him,
> Poor as I am?
> If I were a shepherd
> I would bring a lamb,
> If I were a wise man
> I would do my part—
> Yet what I can, I give Him,
> Give my heart.
>
> CHRISTINA ROSSETTI, "A CHRISTMAS CAROL"

What is one gift I have received that is precious to me? Have I given thanks to the giver for their generosity?

THURSDAY

> Now I know to ask less of them than they can give: a straightforward companionship. And their feelings, their friendship, their generous actions seem in my eyes to be wholly miraculous: a consequence of grace alone.

ALBERT CAMUS, *THE FIRST MAN*

What aspects of myself is Jesus asking me to give freely?

FRIDAY

> Now, Momma said there's only so much fortune a man really needs, and the rest is just for showing off.

FORREST GUMP

What do I truly need in this life? How does Jesus call me to live my life differently so that I may share more generously?

SATURDAY

> Each of you must give as you have made up your mind, not reluctantly or under compulsion, for God loves a cheerful giver.

2 CORINTHIANS 9:7

What constitutes "wealth" in my life? Am I ready to give this wealth away to help another know the love of Jesus more deeply?

Let us pray.

Jesus, you teach us that the widow's gift is the most generous because she gave without limit or fear and from her poverty.

Help me learn from her selfless example that my gifts will bless others beyond measure and will always draw me closer to your heart.

All good things come from you.

I long to offer them with love and no expectations, as the blessed widow did, with trust and perfect hope.

Amen.

WEEK 40

SUNDAY

Gifting Thoughts and Prayers

Jesus Prays for the Church—John 17:1–26

I ask not only on behalf of these, but also on behalf of those who will believe in me through their word, that they may all be one. As you, Father, are in me and I am in you, may they also be in us, so that the world may believe that you have sent me.

JOHN 17:20–21

HAVING IMPARTED MANY TEACHINGS to his disciples, Jesus, in a moment of profound connection, looked up to heaven and prayed for these men he had come to know and love. He beseeched God, with whom he was one, for their protection and sanctification. His prayer was not just a request but a potent catalyst for transformation. He prayed for them as well as for those who might come to know and love him through their words and actions, demonstrating the transformative power of prayer.

When I was a little girl, my go-to gift of choice was the "spiritual bouquet." Since I had no allowance and very little spending money, I would mark special family occasions by hand-crafting a frilly card and filling the center page with a laundry list of promised devotions and actions on behalf of the recipient. For momentous occasions, like my parents' wedding anniversaries, I went big and offered multiple rosaries, sacrifices, and extra acts of help around the house. While I was quick to gift the cards, I wasn't always as diligent about actually fulfilling the promised prayers.

This realization struck me when I hastily posted a brief "thoughts and prayers" message on social media to a good friend who had suffered damage from a natural disaster. My brain released the promise as quickly as I hit "send" on the note. Only when I thought of her later and remembered to quiet my heart and pray for her did I feel a deep sense of accountability and responsibility for fulfilling my promise.

Hearing Jesus beg for his friends' protection must have made them feel unique and beloved. He wasn't just throwing them a prayer-

hands emoji! I long to be the kind of friend who promises prayers and fulfills my desire to help, nurture, and love. I've benefitted from friends like this who remember to check in later after they have lifted me up in prayer. I most desire to give this gift to those in my life who do not yet have a relationship with Jesus. My gift might go unspoken in my desire not to be "that person" who is always preaching like a noisy gong. But with these people, the need to actually deliver on my gift feels all the more pressing.

My Sunday Reflection

How do I feel about genuinely giving my loved ones the gift of praying for them?

MONDAY

> Be good, love the Lord, pray for those who do not know Him. What a great grace it is to know God!
>
> ST. JOSEPHINE BAKHITA

What does giving a loved one the gift of prayer look like in my life?

TUESDAY

> Helped are those whose every act is a prayer for peace; on them depends the future of the world.
>
> ALICE WALKER, *THE TEMPLE OF MY FAMILIAR*

Why does actively praying for others have the potential to change them, me, and our world?

WEDNESDAY

> You give but little when you give of your possessions. It is when you give of yourself that you truly give.
>
> KAHLIL GIBRAN, "ON GIVING"

Where have I sacrificed in my life to actively pray for a friend?

THURSDAY

> Prayer adds an element of surprise to your life that is more fun than a surprise party or surprise gift or surprise romance. In fact, prayer turns life into a party, into a gift, into a romance.
>
> MARK BATTERSON, *THE CIRCLE MAKER*

When can I find time each day to prayerfully remember those I love?

FRIDAY

> It came without ribbons! It came without tags!
> It came without packages, boxes, or bags!
>
> *HOW THE GRINCH STOLE CHRISTMAS*

How might giving a gift of prayer bless and change my relationship with Jesus?

SATURDAY

> Therefore confess your sins to one another, and pray for one another, so that you may be healed. The prayer of the righteous is powerful and effective.
>
> JAMES 5:16

When have I received the gift of prayer? How did it feel?

Let us pray.

Jesus, you tenderly lifted those you loved into the arms of your Father.

You begged for their protection and remembered those whom they would later impact.

Help me to generously give those I care for the gift of prayer as you did.

May my words profess my trust in you.

May my actions testify to my love for them.

Amen.

WEEK 41

SUNDAY

Lost and Found

The Parable of the Lost Sheep—Matthew 18:10–14

What do you think? If a shepherd has a hundred sheep, and one of them has gone astray, does he not leave the ninety-nine on the mountains and go in search of the one that went astray? And if he finds it, truly I tell you, he rejoices over it more than over the ninety-nine that never went astray.

MATTHEW 18:12–13

JESUS OFFERED THE PARABLE OF THE LOST SHEEP, assuring everyone that, like the shepherd who left the ninety-nine in the flock to seek the one lost stray sheep, so too will God seek out those who have gone astray.

My husband and I are opposites in a few ways. His Type A personality traits keep him organized and orderly. I've never known Greg to lose his keys or his wallet. But he has no inherent sense of direction. We can visit a space we've been to many times, but he will still forget the route to our destination.

We complement one another. I am, by nature, quite unorganized. I intentionally wear a watch paired with my phone so that when (not if) my device goes astray, I can locate it. I've worked on being more orderly because it pleases my husband and simplifies life. Unlike Greg, however, I have a built-in GPS and an inborn sense of place.

But I have gotten lost a few times in my adult life. And I have lost things that I could not find, no matter how hard I looked or prayed to St. Anthony, patron saint of lost items. A family heirloom went missing for months following Mom's passing. I wracked my brain to remember if I had been the last to see the treasure. I was sure I hadn't been, but the thought of that lost ring stayed with me. I was overjoyed when it resurfaced.

So, I am consoled by Jesus's reminder that his Father never stops seeking the one lost soul who has strayed from his presence. My life has taken twisty turns. And while I never overtly rejected God, I have known dark nights of the soul where God's presence felt impossibly

distant. I love knowing that just as I never stopped thinking about that lost ring, God always has me in his sights. He seeks me, his beloved. He does the same for anyone whose path has taken them far from Jesus. Not one of us lost sheep will ever be abandoned or forgotten.

My Sunday Reflection

When was the last time I lost my way? How did I feel?

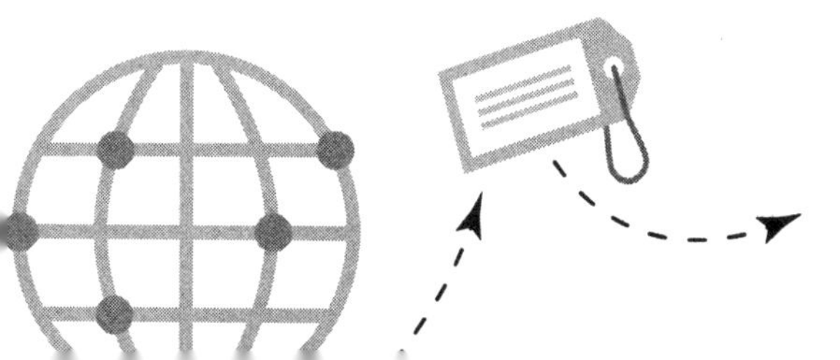

MONDAY

> The shepherd cannot run at the first sign of danger.
>
> BLESSED STANLEY ROTHER

When did I feel Jesus's shepherding presence in a time of peril or fear?

TUESDAY

> He's not trying to find us; He always knows where we are. Rather, He goes with us as we find ourselves again. In this way, we have both a little sheep and some shepherd in us too.
>
> BOB GOFF, *EVERYBODY, ALWAYS*

How have I served as a shepherd to share Jesus's love with someone who was lost?

WEDNESDAY

> This, though I be the feeblest of God's host,
> The sorriest sheep Christ shepherds with His crook.
>
> CHRISTINA ROSSETTI,
> "MONNA INNOMINATA: A SONNET OF SONNETS"

Why do I identify with the lost sheep that Jesus is seeking?

THURSDAY

> Without the Good Shepherd, we are alone in a meaningless story.
>
> PAUL E. MILLER, *A PRAYING LIFE*

How has being found by Jesus become a part of my story?

FRIDAY

> We do not follow maps to buried treasure, and X never, ever, marks the spot.
>
> *INDIANA JONES AND THE LAST CRUSADE*

What most helps me find my way when I feel lost and alone?

SATURDAY

> My people have been lost sheep; their shepherds have led them astray, turning them away on the mountains; from mountain to hill they have gone, they have forgotten their fold.
>
> JEREMIAH 50:6

Who has led me away from Jesus? How can I find my way back to my shepherd?

Let us pray.

Jesus, my Good Shepherd, thank you for the constancy of your love.

When I am lost, please never stop seeking me.

Bless my loved ones who wander.

Gather them into the tenderness and certainty of your embrace.

In you, we are found.

Amen.

WEEK 42

SUNDAY

In Doubt and Desolation

Jesus Prays in Gethsemane—Mark 14:32–42

He came a third time and said to them, “Are you still sleeping and taking your rest? Enough! The hour has come; the Son of Man is betrayed into the hands of sinners. Get up, let us be going. See, my betrayer is at hand.”

MARK 14:41–42

JESUS LED HIS DISCIPLES TO GETHSEMANE, asking them to sit with him while he prayed. Taking Peter, James, and John with him, he shared his feelings with them and then stepped away to a quiet spot to pray by himself. Jesus called on his Father, praying that if it was God's desire, he might be spared the fate he knew awaited him. But he also expressed his conviction to do his Father's will. Three times he checked on his friends, who slept as he prayed in anguish.

I have known a few moments of extreme desolation where the excruciating nature of my emotional pain felt unbearable. Once, my despair was so deep that I could not find the words or mental strength to pray for myself. In the looming darkness, I lost all hope. I wandered in a mental haze for a few days before finally confessing to my husband that I felt I was in severe physical and emotional danger. He listened intently, never dismissing my feelings. He held my hand literally and figuratively, helping me find solace and aid. Knowing I was not alone in that moment meant everything to me.

I have also been on the other side of helping a friend who experienced extreme despair. The depth of her pain frightened me, but I knew that I could not walk away in her moment of need. I sought the help I needed to support her and keep her secure. I also surrounded both of us with prayer, my own as well as the prayers of trusted friends I asked confidentially for help.

I recall visiting Gethsemane on the Mount of Olives during my pilgrimage to the Holy Land. The gnarled, knotty olive trees that grow in that holy space stood watch during Jesus's passion and sense of abandonment. Standing among them, I was struck by Jesus's

expression of his human doubt and isolation. Not once or twice but *three* times he returned to his friends and found them asleep. Despite his pleas that they keep watch, the disciples let him down by literally sleeping on the job. How often have I "slept on" a friend's needs? Jesus calls me to accompany those who despair. Jesus hears my cries of pain because he cried his own. And Jesus knows my doubts and loves me in spite of them.

My Sunday Reflection

When have I experienced desolation? How did I seek help?

MONDAY

> The most holy passion of Jesus is a sea of sorrows but, at the same time, a sea of love. Pray to God that he teach you to fish in the sea; then dive into its depths. No matter how deep you go, you will never reach the bottom. Allow yourself to be penetrated completely by sorrow and love.

ST. PAUL OF THE CROSS,
THE MYSTICISM OF THE PASSION IN ST. PAUL OF THE CROSS

How does allowing myself to be in touch with my pain draw me closer to Jesus?

TUESDAY

> Peter had believed. Peter had doubted. Peter had asked for help, and had been saved. Certainly, at that moment, the fisherman from Bethsaida could not have imagined the immense number of people in every corner of the earth in the centuries yet to come, who would live that same experience, even without walking on water.

ANDREA TORNIELLI, *THE LIFE OF JESUS*

What can I do when my doubts paralyze me?

WEDNESDAY

> I wake, doubt, beside you,
> like a curtain half-open.

JANE HIRSHFIELD, "MY DOUBT"

How does knowing that Jesus doubted help me understand his love for me?

THURSDAY

> In Gethsemane the holiest of all petitioners prayed
> three times that a certain cup might pass from Him.
> It did not.

C. S. LEWIS, *THE WORLD'S LAST NIGHT AND OTHER ESSAYS*

Where is my own personal Gethsemane? Have I ever asked God, as Jesus did, to spare me from a trial or moment of pain?

FRIDAY

> I would have followed you, my brother, my captain,
> my king.

J. R. R. TOLKIEN, *THE FELLOWSHIP OF THE RING*

How have I chosen to follow Jesus, confident of his love for me?

SATURDAY

> Why are you cast down, O my soul,
> and why are you disquieted within me?
> Hope in God; for I shall again praise him,
> my help and my God.

PSALM 43:5

What words of prayer in times of despair help me feel Jesus's nearness to me?

Let us pray.

**Jesus, in your moment of distress and pain,
you prayed.**

**Turning to your beloved Father, you expressed
your fears but accepted his will.**

**Even when your friends disappointed you,
you gave your life for them and me.**

**Wrap me in your embrace when desolation
blankets me.**

Forgive my doubts.

May your will, not mine, be done in my life.

Amen.

WEEK 43

SUNDAY

In Memory of Jesus

Jesus Institutes the Eucharist—Luke 22:14–23

Then he took a loaf of bread, and when he had given thanks, he broke it and gave it to them, saying, "This is my body, which is given for you. Do this in remembrance of me." And he did the same with the cup after supper, saying, "This cup that is poured out for you is the new covenant in my blood."

LUKE 22:19–20

JESUS CALLED HIS DISCIPLES AROUND HIM to share the Passover meal. Fully aware that this would be his final sustenance, he took a cup of wine and shared it with them. Then, taking the bread, he gave thanks and broke it. He said that the bread was his body, broken for them, and the cup his blood, shed for them. He invited them to do this in memory of him. All the while, Jesus knew that his betrayer sat among them.

For me, as a Catholic follower of Jesus, the Eucharist is the cornerstone of my faith. We Catholics believe that at the moment of transubstantiation, the bread and wine truly become the body and blood of Christ. By consuming the Eucharist, we unite with our Lord, Jesus, and reaffirm our faith in his sacrifice and the significance of the Eucharist in our lives. In memory of Jesus, we are united with those worldwide who love and serve him and one another.

Those of us who live in families know the beauty of a family meal. United at the table, we tell stories, debate topics of importance, laugh over shared encounters, and linger in joyful love with one another. Imperfect as we are, we each bring something unique to the table. When we say our goodbyes, the food we have shared and the memories we have made become a part of the individuals we are going forward.

I am not a theologian capable of expositing all the mysteries of the Eucharist. I am a simple woman. But I know that my life has been changed through my belief in Jesus and by his presence within me. I have had the gift of gathering for communion in hundreds of churches worldwide. Regardless of the presiding priest's language,

I know exactly what happens during the Eucharistic prayers. Holy Communion is a family meal that occurs at every hour of every day. We come together to remember Jesus's profound love for us and his sacrifice. We gather to profess our faith and receive him within ourselves. We depart, sent to be the body and blood of Christ to all we encounter—those who need to know Jesus's love and ours, too. By remembering him in this way, we transform ourselves and our world.

My Sunday Reflection

What helps me remember the sacrifice Jesus made for me?

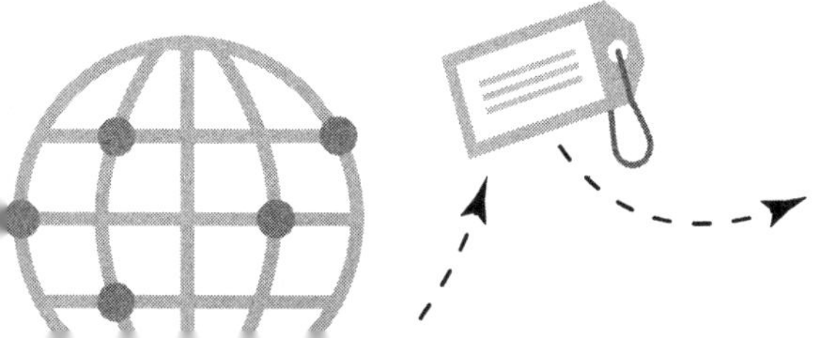

MONDAY

> Go often to Holy Communion. Go very often! This is your one remedy.

ST. THÉRÈSE OF LISIEUX, *THE LETTERS OF ST. THÉRÈSE OF LISIEUX*

How often do I pause to remember Jesus's love for me?

TUESDAY

> We seldom notice how each day is a holy place
> Where the eucharist of the ordinary happens.

JOHN O'DONOHUE,
TO BLESS THE SPACE BETWEEN US: A BOOK OF BLESSINGS

How has being transformed by Jesus changed the way I live my life and how I see the world around me?

WEDNESDAY

> Remember me when I am gone away,
> Gone far away into the silent land;
> When you can no more hold me by the hand,
> Nor I half turn to go yet turning stay.

CHRISTINA ROSSETTI, "REMEMBER"

When I remember Jesus, how do I feel?

THURSDAY

> The word "Eucharist" means literally "act of thanksgiving." To celebrate the Eucharist and to live a Eucharistic life has everything to do with gratitude. Living Eucharistically is living life as a gift, a gift for which one is grateful.

HENRI J. M. NOUWEN,
WITH BURNING HEARTS: A MEDITATION ON THE EUCHARISTIC LIFE

How do I share my gratitude for Jesus's love?

FRIDAY

> Remember me.

COCO

Why does intentionally remembering Jesus matter to me?

SATURDAY

> So, whether you eat or drink, or whatever you do, do everything for the glory of God.

1 CORINTHIANS 10:31

When have I lived intentionally for Jesus? What did this look like?

Let us pray.

Jesus, in memory of you, we take bread and wine and share them.

You become a part of me through these gifts, transforming me with your saving body and blood.

As you gathered those you love close to your heart, draw me to you.

Fill me to overflowing with your love so I may share it with everyone I meet.

May my hunger and thirst for your true presence never be satisfied.

Live in me.

Amen.

WEEK 44

SUNDAY

Rising Again

The Resurrection of Jesus—John 20:1–10

Then Simon Peter came, following him, and went into the tomb. He saw the linen wrappings lying there, and the cloth that had been on Jesus' head, not lying with the linen wrappings but rolled up in a place by itself. Then the other disciple, who reached the tomb first, also went in, and he saw and believed; for as yet they did not understand the scripture, that he must rise from the dead.

JOHN 20:6–9

MARY MAGDALENE DISCOVERED THAT JESUS'S BODY was no longer in the tomb. She ran to tell Simon Peter and John. Both men then ran to the tomb. They found the tomb empty, and the linens neatly folded. John saw and believed.

When I linger with John's writings on the Resurrection, I am struck by the amount of *running* in these verses. Mary, discovering the absence of her beloved master, runs to tell the leaders she trusts. Simon Peter and John then run together to the tomb. John makes a point of telling us that he arrived first but he allows Peter to enter before him. All of this running conveys both anxiousness and excitement. Those who have loved Jesus during his earthly ministry are grieving. They fear. And yet, a glimmer of hope fills them with the need to see for themselves. So they run with every ounce of energy they have. Not fully understanding what has happened, they must share with others what they have experienced.

Have you ever encountered something that knocked you off your chosen path? I experienced a sense of this with my cancer journey. The weeks and months after my surgery and radiation treatments felt like being locked in a cave. My body and spirit needed recuperation. When I was finally able to enter the world again, I felt keen gratitude. My heart was ready for what came next. I couldn't wait to run, albeit slowly, into what my future held.

The miracle of Jesus's resurrection is hard for our human brains to process. One moment, Jesus is dead, and his beloved friends are reeling from the loss. The next, he has victoriously risen, no longer bound. They see and believe. Their lives are inexorably changed. They must run to tell the world!

You and I will not experience someone's bodily resurrection in our lifetimes, but we hope in the joy of new life with Jesus. We are gifted some tiny sense of resurrection by recognizing small moments when we, too, "rise again" by God's grace, overcoming trials, burdens, or defeats, emerging to embrace God's will. Rising, we are invited into the hope of what is yet to come. We can run into what awaits us by linking our "small risings" with the power of the Resurrection. We will see and believe.

My Sunday Reflection

How would I have felt when I saw Jesus's empty tomb that morning?

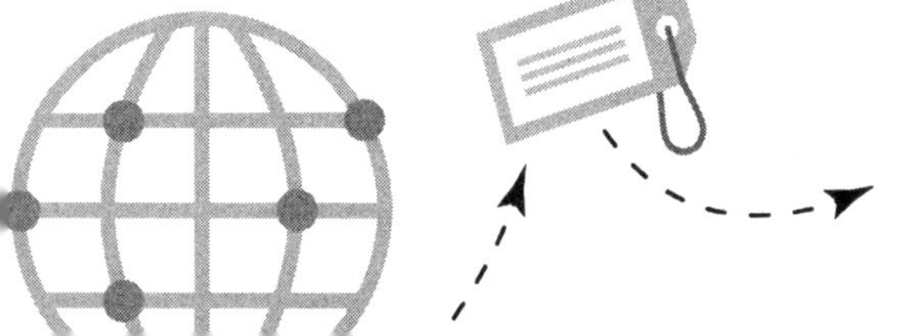

MONDAY

> Why should we today sing Alleluia, Praise the Lord?
> Because this day we are fed, freed, assured of the truth,
> and given promises of being endowed, in our resurrection,
> with the gifts of clarity, agility, brightness and
> impassibility, which Christ showed in his resurrection.

ST. VINCENT FERRER, "SERMON 2 ON EASTER"

How does Jesus's resurrection free me to live more fully for him?

TUESDAY

> This promise of resurrection is our hope. It is that on which we stake our life. It is what enables us, as Christians, to face death with courage and joy.

SCOTT HAHN, *HOPE TO DIE: THE CHRISTIAN MEANING OF DEATH AND THE RESURRECTION OF THE BODY*

When has the hope I feel in Jesus helped me to face defeats in my life?

WEDNESDAY

> Just like hopes springing high,
> Still I'll rise.

MAYA ANGELOU, "STILL I RISE"

How is Jesus inviting me to rise up anew in his love?

THURSDAY

> In spite of everything I shall rise again: I will take up my pencil, which I have forsaken in my great discouragement, and I will go on with my drawing.

VINCENT VAN GOGH, "*VINCENT TO HIS BROTHER THEO,*"
FRIDAY, 24 SEPTEMBER 1880

What discouragement am I facing? How will Jesus help me rise up with renewed conviction?

FRIDAY

> Rise and rise again until lambs become lions.

ROBIN HOOD (2010)

What helps me continue rising again in the face of challenge?

SATURDAY

> Blessed be the God and Father of our Lord Jesus Christ! By his great mercy he has given us a new birth into a living hope through the resurrection of Jesus Christ from the dead.

1 PETER 1:3

Knowing that Jesus rose from the dead to give me hope, how do I feel?

Let us pray.

Jesus, you rose into the glory of new life.

Your resurrection gave hope to your followers and sent them running to the ends of the earth to share your story.

Arise in me, Lord.

Help me believe in the hope of your promise.

Fill me with zeal to be your love to a world too often buried in despair.

I see you, Jesus, and I believe.

Amen.

WEEK 45

SUNDAY

When Everyone Wins

The Laborers in the Vineyard—Matthew 20:1–16

Am I not allowed to do what I choose with what belongs to me? Or are you envious because I am generous? So the last will be first, and the first will be last.

MATTHEW 20:15–16

JESUS TOLD HIS FOLLOWERS a story about laborers in a vineyard. The landowner hired the first set of workers early in the morning. They agreed on a fair daily wage and went straight to work. Throughout the day, the landowner hired additional laborers. When the time came to compensate his workforce, he paid them all an equal wage. Those who had worked all day grumbled self-righteously. But as was his prerogative, the landowner reminded them that, ultimately, the decision was his. He would not be begrudged for his generosity.

Growing up as the eldest of five, I had a heightened sense of fairness that often demonstrated as jealousy. My father loved to play games of his own creation with us. But he had one hard-and-fast rule: "One tie, all tie." Everyone won the game if two or more siblings finished with the same score. Since Daddy was in charge of the rules, he always tried to create a tied-score scenario. It continuously infuriated me that my earned victory would be snatched from my grasp at the last minute by my baby brother.

I realize now that Daddy was busy teaching us important lessons about justice, compassion, and generosity. When I became a parent, I implemented my own version of "one tie, all tie." Of course, I wanted my sons, whom I loved equally, to know the joy of succeeding and being rewarded!

Unfortunately, by nature, I tend to mentally side with the hardworking laborers who started their day at the crack of dawn and felt they deserved a bonus. As someone with an overly diligent work ethic, I show up early, give my best, and hope that my efforts are noticed. Acknowledging these traits about myself doesn't make me proud.

But understanding that the most incredible "prize" in this parable is knowing the saving love of Jesus softens my heart. We who feel Jesus's divine presence in the stuff of our daily lives should want this same joy for everyone we know. It's never too late to be welcomed into the fullness of God's grace, freely extended to each of us regardless of our worthiness. In Jesus's kingdom, there is room for everyone to win.

My Sunday Reflection

Which group of laborers do I identify with? Why?

MONDAY

> You are rewarded not according to time or work but according to the measure of your love.

ST. CATHERINE OF SIENA, *THE DIALOGUE OF THE SERAPHIC VIRGIN, CATHERINE OF SIENA*

What is Jesus saying to me in this parable?

TUESDAY

> To believe your own thought, to believe that what is true for you in your private heart, is true for all men,—that is genius.

RALPH WALDO EMERSON, *SELF-RELIANCE*

When have I been grateful for the grace Jesus extends to others?

WEDNESDAY

> A little counts for much with Him we serve,
> And yet, ungenerous, grasping, we reserve
> Our claim for recompense adequate, and more
> Than he receives who brings a lesser store!

CHARLOTTE MASON, *THE SAVIOUR OF THE WORLD*

Why do I want others to know the joy of being loved by Jesus?

THURSDAY

> We fear to come in second or third or last. We fear to fall from grace or to be found wanting. Our own lacking makes us angry—at ourselves, others, and the world. And when we are stuck in a fog of rage, we make everyone miserable. That's the trap.

ERIC A. CLAYTON,
MY LIFE WITH THE JEDI: THE SPIRITUALITY OF STAR WARS

When have I placed the needs of others above my own? How did I feel?

FRIDAY

> Beethoven was deaf. Helen Keller was blind. I think Rocky's got a good chance.

ROCKY

Where did Jesus meet me when I was the last to be chosen, and help me feel special?

SATURDAY

> For by grace you have been saved through faith, and this is not your own doing; it is the gift of God—not the result of works, so that no one may boast.

EPHESIANS 2:8–9

How is Jesus saving me by his grace, through no merit of my own?

Let us pray.

Jesus, there is endless room for those you love in your kingdom.

You call us to you regardless of our inability to earn your saving grace.

Thank you for your embrace, which knows no limits or barriers.

Help me extend my hand to accompany those who long for love.

May I always lead them home to you, where all are welcomed.

Amen.

WEEK 46

SUNDAY

Laying Loved Ones to Rest

The Burial of Jesus—Mark 15:42–47

When evening had come, and since it was the day of Preparation, that is, the day before the sabbath, Joseph of Arimathea, a respected member of the council, who was also himself waiting expectantly for the kingdom of God, took courage and went boldly to Pilate, and asked for the body of Jesus.

MARK 15:42–43

ON THE EVENING OF THE DAY OF PREPARATION before the Sabbath, Joseph of Arimathea went to Pilate to request Jesus's body. Pilate consulted with a centurion and then released the body to Joseph. Wrapping it in linen shrouds, Joseph placed it in a rocky tomb and rolled a stone in front of it. Mary Magdalene and the other Mary took special care to see where Jesus was buried as they honored the body of their deceased loved one.

As I age and contemplate my mortality, I've grown to love the rites and rituals surrounding the burial of the dead. I don't say this in a macabre fashion. I am not fascinated with death. But my own experiences of the deaths of my parents have redefined my thinking about laying our loved ones to rest.

A few years before my parents became infirm, we journeyed to their hometown of Fort Wayne, Indiana, visiting their childhood homes, their parishes, the high school where they met, and their parents' grave sites. The timing was fortuitous. During our cemetery visits, we discussed our funerals and burial preferences. I learned that my mother strongly preferred to be laid to rest near the spot Greg and I had already chosen: a lovely mausoleum at our alma mater, the University of Notre Dame. Only a few years after this conversation, we were laying our parents to rest there.

Burying the dead is a corporal work of mercy, a direct response to Jesus's teachings. His own loved ones did this for their teacher and friend. Joseph of Arimathea was a wealthy, respected council member, a disciple who truly loved Jesus. I understand now that the act of burying his friend was probably critical to Joseph's grieving process, because I found the beginnings of my own healing as I attended to the details of my parents' burials.

When we visit our parents in their resting spot, I spend time praying for the repose of their souls. I imagine Joseph, Nicodemus, Mary Magdalene, and the other Mary did this very thing near Jesus's rocky tomb. But I also contemplate my future burial right beside Mom and Daddy, with Greg. Being in that sacred place now brings me joy. I trust that my parents rest in Jesus's embrace. God willing, someday I will too.

My Sunday Reflection

How do I feel as I imagine Joseph of Arimathea laying Jesus in his tomb?

MONDAY

> Live so as not to fear death. For those who live well in the world, death is not frightening but sweet and precious.

ST. ROSE OF VITERBO

When I anticipate my eventual death, how does it draw me closer to Jesus?

TUESDAY

> The pain of grief is just as much a part of life as the joy of love; it is, perhaps, the price we pay for love, the cost of commitment.

COLIN MURRAY PARKES AND HOLLY G. PRIGERSON,
BEREAVEMENT: STUDIES OF GRIEF IN ADULT LIFE

Who, living or dead, am I grieving at this time in my life?

WEDNESDAY

> Life is real! Life is earnest!
>   And the grave is not its goal;
> Dust thou art, to dust returnest,
>   Was not spoken of the soul.

HENRY WADSWORTH LONGFELLOW,
"VOICES OF THE NIGHT: A PSALM OF LIFE"

What has Jesus taught me by his death and resurrection?

THURSDAY

> The road to death, in reality, is a way of hope and it passes through our cemeteries, just as can be read on the tombstones, and fulfills a journey marked by the hope of eternity.

POPE BENEDICT XVI, "COMMEMORATION OF ALL THE FAITHFUL DEPARTED," GENERAL AUDIENCE, NOVEMBER 2, 2011

How did burying or saying goodbye to someone I love help me reach out to Jesus with hope for eternity?

FRIDAY

> I don't even remember what it was I was mad about and I don't care. Whatever it was that you did, I forgive you.

BEACHES

What unrepented anger can I hand over to Jesus?

SATURDAY

> The sting of death is sin, and the power of sin is the law. But thanks be to God, who gives us the victory through our Lord Jesus Christ.

1 CORINTHIANS 15:56–57

Why does loving Jesus give me victory over the sting of death?

Let us pray.

Jesus, after your terrible Passion and death, your friend Joseph cared for your mortal body.

With tenderness, he laid you in his tomb.

Although that space could never contain your divinity, your loved ones sought you there.

Help me minister to the dead and grieving with the same tenderness Joseph showed.

May I always anticipate my death and pray for eternal life with you.

Amen.

WEEK 47

SUNDAY

Jesus, Remember Me

The Crucifixion of Jesus—Luke 23:26–43

Then he said, "Jesus, remember me when you come into your kingdom." He replied, "Truly I tell you, today you will be with me in Paradise."

LUKE 23:42–43

JESUS CARRIED HIS CROSS, aided at times by Simon of Cyrene, and comforted women who wept for him. At Golgotha, soldiers carried out preparations to put Jesus to death by crucifixion, placing him between two criminals. One of the criminals challenged Jesus to save himself and them. But the other humbly begged Jesus to remember him when he came into his power. Jesus assured this man that he would be with Jesus in paradise.

We commonly refer to the man who admitted his sinfulness before Jesus as the "Good Thief, Dismas." Unlike the unrepentant criminal who hung on the other side of Jesus, or the soldiers who cast lots for Jesus's garments, or the people who had mocked him, Dismas, believing in Jesus's divinity, humbled himself. When Jesus assured Dismas of an eternity spent with him in heaven, Jesus in effect was giving the same assurance to all of us who beg our Lord to call us to himself.

During the liturgy for Palm Sunday, the Feast of the Lord's Passion, when the church reads from the Gospel according to Luke, I am often moved to tears by the words of the Good Thief. The Taizé community, an ecumenical community in France, has gifted us a hymn composed solely of his words, "Jesus, remember me when you come into your kingdom." Meditating upon the Passion always reminds me of my part in his death. What would I have done had I stood on Golgotha that day? Would I have cowered in fear, crowed retributions, or cried in humble recognition of this man's divinity?

Today, we encounter many "good thieves" who overcome a lifetime of evil, misfortune, or lack of knowledge to discover, in the glimmer of an instant, the unshakeable mercy of Jesus Christ. The lifelong alcoholic who chooses sobriety, the family members

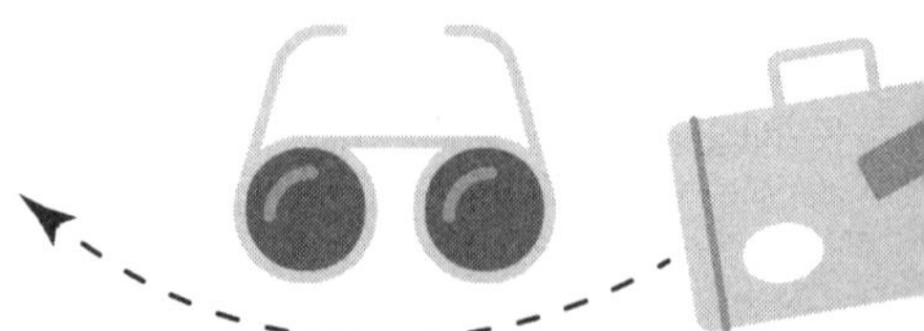

who end a decades-long feud, and the death-row convict who pronounces a last-minute belief each have something to teach me about the hope that is to be found in Jesus. If they can embrace the power of conversion, it is promised to me, too, despite my perceived unworthiness.

Jesus did not run from his cross. Out of love, he embraced it fully. But he went to his death still seeking ways to help us believe what his Father had sent him to teach: the power of love.

My Sunday Reflection

What would I ask of Jesus at the moment of his crucifixion?

MONDAY

> The greater the sinner, the greater the right he has to my mercy.

JESUS TO ST. FAUSTINA, *DIARY OF ST. FAUSTINA*

How do I feel when contemplating Jesus's mercy for me?

TUESDAY

> I hope to see my friend and shake his hand. I hope the Pacific is as blue as it has been in my dreams. I hope.

STEPHEN KING,
RITA HAYWORTH AND THE SHAWSHANK REDEMPTION

What are my hopes for life beyond this life?

WEDNESDAY

> For Mercy has a human heart,
> Pity a human face,
> And Love, the human form divine,
> And Peace, the human dress.

WILLIAM BLAKE, "THE DIVINE IMAGE"

When have I been a source of mercy for someone else?

THURSDAY

> It is better that ten guilty persons escape than that one innocent suffer.
>
> WILLIAM BLACKSTONE,
> *COMMENTARIES ON THE LAWS OF ENGLAND*

What do I believe about the chance for conversion to Jesus's love?

FRIDAY

> I want the last face you see in this world to be the face of love, so you look at me when they do this thing. I'll be the face of love for you.
>
> *DEAD MAN WALKING*

How have I been the face of love for someone who needs to know Jesus?

SATURDAY

> The LORD is merciful and gracious,
> slow to anger and abounding in steadfast love.
>
> PSALM 103:8

Why is Jesus's steadfast love so important in my life?

Let us pray.

Jesus, you went to your death with human emotion and divine power.

By embracing your fate, you teach me to face my crosses with faith and trust.

Thank you for loving me so much that you would suffer unspeakable pain on my behalf.

Jesus, remember me when you come into your kingdom.

Amen.

SUNDAY

Not Seeing Yet Believing

Jesus and Thomas—John 20:24–29

Now Thomas (who was called the Twin), one of the twelve, was not with them when Jesus came. So the other disciples told him, "We have seen the Lord." But he said to them, "Unless I see the mark of the nails in his hands, and place my finger in the mark of the nails and my hand in his side, I will not believe."

JOHN 20:24–25

WHEN THE OTHER DISCIPLES told Thomas they had encountered Jesus, he refused to believe them. He would accept their word only if he himself could touch Jesus. Eight days later, Jesus appeared to the group again; this time, Thomas was present. Jesus confronted him, inviting him to touch and believe. Then, he blessed all those who would never see but would choose to believe.

We read that when Thomas saw Jesus with his own eyes, he immediately responded, "My Lord and my God!" I was brought up in my Catholic family and school to whisper these exact words in the silence of my heart during the consecration when the priest elevates the host and the chalice during the Mass. "My Lord and my God" is my reflexive, silent response at every Mass. Even when I am distracted, the ringing of brass altar bells during the moment of the transubstantiation summons me back into a moment of presence. The words are in my heart.

Too often, I profess with my lips, but my actions speak another story. I play a game of "show me" with Jesus, offering him my laundry list of prayer intentions and asking him to prove himself by granting me access to personal signs of his love. I negotiate with him: *I will believe more fervently when you take care of XYZ, Lord.* When I catch myself engaging in this Thomistic behavior, I pray the words of the father in Mark 9:24, "I believe; help my unbelief!" I will spend my lifetime striving to overcome doubt as Thomas did. And yet, I persist.

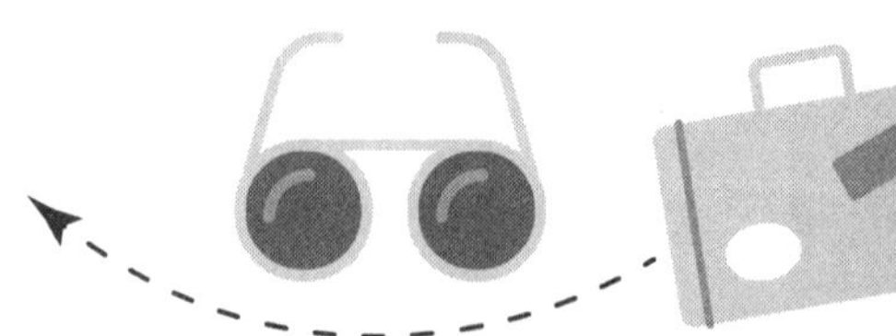

Living this kind of faith journey has helped me walk alongside those who do not share my beliefs. I recognize that each of us has our path in this life. In the past, I have made the grave mistake of trying to force my faith on others. Many times have I regretted and repented doing this. Now, I ask Jesus for the grace to walk with others wherever they are. May we all one day know Jesus's peace, setting aside our hopelessness and discovering belief in his unfailing love for us, each in our way.

My Sunday Reflection

What has helped me overcome moments of doubt in Jesus's love?

MONDAY

> Believe in the whisperings of God to your own heart.
>
> ST. MARY OF THE CROSS MACKILLOP

When has Jesus whispered something into my heart?

TUESDAY

> We can help one another to find out the meaning of life, no doubt. But in the last analysis the individual person is responsible for living his own life and for "finding himself."
>
> THOMAS MERTON, *NO MAN IS AN ISLAND*

How have I come to understand the meaning of my life in Jesus?

WEDNESDAY

> But to have a dark night
> One must have first had a bright day.
>
> JUSTIN FARLEY, "DARK NIGHT OF THE SOUL"

What has helped me recognize that I am truly never alone?

THURSDAY

> In the realist, faith is not born from miracles, but miracles from faith. Once the realist comes to believe, then, precisely because of his realism, he must also allow for miracles.

FYODOR DOSTOEVSKY, *THE BROTHERS KARAMAZOV*

Where have I encountered small miracles through the grace of believing in Jesus?

FRIDAY

> Seeing is believing, but sometimes the most real things in the world are the things we can't see.

THE POLAR EXPRESS

What are some things I believe but cannot see?

SATURDAY

> When I thought, "My foot is slipping,"
> your steadfast love, O LORD, held me up.
> When the cares of my heart are many,
> your consolations cheer my soul.

PSALM 94:18–19

When has the love of Jesus held me up in moments of pain and doubt?

Let us pray.

Jesus, you met Thomas on his terms, offering him the chance to honestly believe by inviting him into a personal encounter.

Help me open my heart to you, Lord.

Meet me in my moments of faithlessness and doubt.

Transform me into the kind of believer who helps others truly know your love's grace.

Amen.

WEEK 49

SUNDAY

Denial and Remorse

Peter Denies Jesus—Matthew 26:69–75

Then he began to curse, and he swore an oath, "I do not know the man!" At that moment the cock crowed. Then Peter remembered what Jesus had said: "Before the cock crows, you will deny me three times." And he went out and wept bitterly.

MATTHEW 26:74–75

WHILE JESUS UNDERWENT HIS TRIAL before Caiaphas, Peter sat fearfully in a courtyard. Three people accused him of being an associate of Jesus, and he vehemently denied any relationship. Peter wept bitterly after the third denial, remembering how Jesus had foretold his actions.

As parents, we learn to read the hidden expressions of our children. The curl of a lip, the sideways glance, or a silence that lasts just a bit too long can all be "tells" that help a parent see inside the soul of their little one. As they grow, it becomes more challenging to anticipate the hidden secrets that might harm our children. Yet intuitively, we often know.

Praying over Peter's denials reminds me of the first sin I knowingly committed as a child. My mother took me to purchase a new lunch box. I had my eye on a model with a bonus set of magnets. Mom had her eye on our budget, which didn't account for this luxury. When she wasn't looking, I swiped the magnets and placed them inside the budget version she had chosen. Arriving home, Mom discovered my thievery. She led me back to the store and had me return the magnets and apologize. I recall initially denying my behavior and then crying profusely when the truth came out. It was the first and last time I ever stole something. But when I remember that day, the remorse still burns in my stomach.

Often, our acts of denying Jesus's love are far more subtle. We camouflage ourselves in groups to hide our true political, social, or religious identities to fit in. We laugh at off-color jokes while squirming inside. We pretend to disavow a friend so that we are accepted. Any time I find myself behaving in one of these ways, I immediately share

the shame Peter must have known that night in the courtyard when the cock crowed three times. But Scripture reminds me that Jesus not only extended mercy to Peter but also chose Peter to carry his message of salvific love to the ends of the earth. In our humanity, we sometimes fail, but in his love, Jesus embraces us, forgives us, and sends us out to treat others with the same mercy he offered to Peter. Sin is not the end of our story. In, with, and through Jesus, we encounter the cross, our greatest hope.

My Sunday Reflection

When have I knowingly denied Jesus?
Have I repented of this to repair my relationship with Jesus?

MONDAY

No one, however weak, is denied a share in the victory of the cross. No one is beyond the help of the prayer of Christ.

ST. LEO THE GREAT

What helps me believe in the saving love of Jesus?

TUESDAY

Chronic remorse, as all the moralists are agreed, is a most undesirable sentiment. If you have behaved badly, repent, make what amends you can and address yourself to the task of behaving better next time.

ALDOUS HUXLEY, *BRAVE NEW WORLD*

What act for which I feel chronic remorse do I need to repent?

WEDNESDAY

For each man kills the thing he loves,
Yet each man does not die.

OSCAR WILDE, "THE BALLAD OF READING GAOL"

Why has past denial or regret kept me from being closer to Jesus?

THURSDAY

> How many are there now in existence who, not from any humility, but from mere apprehension of what the world will say, are afraid to own any Christian or virtuous action and to profess themselves followers of Christ!

ROGER BAXTER, *MEDITATIONS FOR EVERY DAY IN THE YEAR*

Why am I sometimes afraid to let others know I love and follow Jesus?

FRIDAY

> Never look behind, only ahead.

THE MESSENGER: THE STORY OF JOAN OF ARC

How can I look forward and beyond my broken nature to better love and serve others?

SATURDAY

> Whoever says, "I am in the light," while hating a brother or sister, is still in the darkness. Whoever loves a brother or sister lives in the light, and in such a person there is no cause for stumbling.

1 JOHN 2:9–10

What helps me believe that Jesus truly loves and forgives me when I have fallen short?

Let us pray.

Jesus, your chosen disciple Peter knowingly denied you as you faced trial and persecution.

You foretold his sins, yet you also chose him to lead all of us in coming to know and love you.

Forgive my acts and words of denial.

Embolden me to share my love for you with courage, kindness, and sensitivity.

Amen.

WEEK 50

SUNDAY

Equipping the Called

Jesus Commissions the Disciples—Mark 16:14–18

Later he appeared to the eleven themselves as they were sitting at the table; and he upbraided them for their lack of faith and stubbornness, because they had not believed those who saw him after he had risen. And he said to them, "Go into all the world and proclaim the good news to the whole creation."

MARK 16:14–15

MARK WRITES that following his resurrection, Jesus appeared to Mary Magdalene, to two of his disciples as they walked, and then to the eleven as they sat at the table. Initially, Jesus chastised everyone for their lack of belief. But then Jesus commissioned his followers, sending them out to share the Good News. He offered them signs by which their new followers would know their beliefs.

I hold a few volunteer positions that have involved being "commissioned" for service. In every case, the commissioning involved a public inquiry about my willingness to accept the rules of service, followed by a public proclamation of my readiness to serve. In almost every situation, I assented publicly while feeling some amount of trepidation about my worthiness. And in all but one situation, things seemed to work themselves out.

A quotation is commonly used in Christian circles: "God doesn't call the equipped; he equips the called." While I can't find the source for this wisdom, I've seen it apply to everything from marriage prep to committee recruitment in parish circles. I've also used it myself while encouraging others to step into the challenge of publicly sharing their faith in Jesus. I didn't begin this work because I had all the answers about being a follower of Christ. I stumbled into it because I was seeking answers and companionship along the journey. I would also likely have been upbraided by Jesus for my lack of conviction. But just as Jesus sent his disciples out with instructions, so, too, has he led my path toward him.

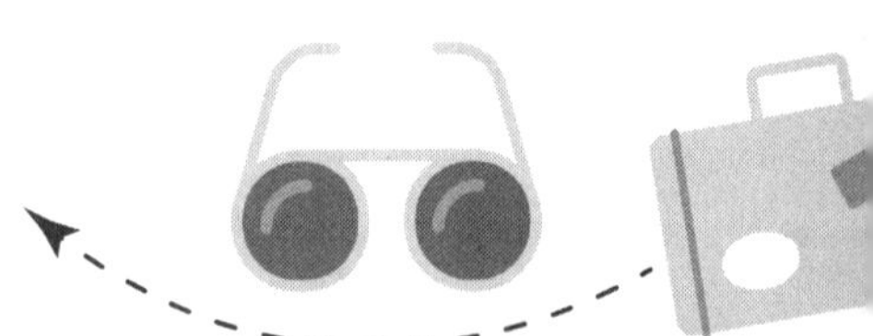

Over my years of ministry involvement, I've grown increasingly honest about my fears, doubts, and lack of knowledge. I never want to come across as holier than thou, nor do I want anyone to believe that I am a perfect Christian. But being honest about this and sharing how much the love of Jesus has blessed me is often a great place to begin a conversation about faith. Like the disciples, who at one time or another expressed fear or disbelief, my genuine human sentiments help me hear the hearts of those Jesus has sent me to serve. I'm confident he will also equip me for whatever lies ahead.

My Sunday Reflection

For what purpose has Jesus commissioned me to live my life?

MONDAY

> Be sure that you first preach by the way you live. If you do not, people will notice that you say one thing, but live otherwise, and your words will bring only cynical laughter and a derisive shake of the head.

ST. CHARLES BORROMEO, *APHORISMS*

How does the way I live my life reveal what I want to share about Jesus?

TUESDAY

> God isn't impressed by fancy titles or Ivy League degrees. He's impressed by how faithfully we carry out the work he's entrusted to us. That work always has eternal significance, even if it seems to be of little temporal importance.

EMILY STIMPSON,
THE CATHOLIC GIRL'S SURVIVAL GUIDE FOR THE SINGLE YEARS

Why has Jesus commissioned me to share his love?

WEDNESDAY

> O Divine Master,
> Grant that I may not so much seek
> to be consoled as to console;
> To be understood as to understand;
> To be loved as to love;
> For it is in giving that we receive.

ST. FRANCIS OF ASSISI, "PRAYER FOR PEACE"

When have I made it a priority to share with someone that Jesus loves them?

THURSDAY

> Christianity is not a set of private convictions that we cultivate inwardly or whisper among ourselves. It is the message that the whole world needs to hear. We who have heard it must become agents of subversion and transformation.
>
> ROBERT BARRON, *EXPLORING CATHOLIC THEOLOGY*

Where is Jesus sending me to speak truth and transformation?

FRIDAY

> Young man, sometimes the right path is not the easiest one. Don't you see?
>
> *POCAHONTAS*

What is challenging about sharing my love for Jesus? Why do I do it anyway?

SATURDAY

> But even if you do suffer for doing what is right, you are blessed. Do not fear what they fear, and do not be intimidated, but in your hearts sanctify Christ as Lord. Always be ready to make your defense to anyone who demands from you an accounting for the hope that is in you.
>
> 1 PETER 3:14–15

What is my reason for hope in Jesus?

Let us pray.

Jesus, you sent your disciples to share the good news of your love.

None of them was perfect, yet you used them to reach into the hearts of millions.

Equip me, Lord, to serve as you are calling me.

Correct in me any sin or shortcoming that would keep others from knowing your love.

I will preach the words you place into my soul.

I will go where you send me.

Amen.

WEEK 51

SUNDAY

Walking with Jesus

The Walk to Emmaus—Luke 24:13–35

Now on that same day two of them were going to a village called Emmaus, about seven miles from Jerusalem, and talking with each other about all these things that had happened. While they were talking and discussing, Jesus himself came near and went with them.

LUKE 24:13–15

AFTER JESUS'S TOMB WAS DISCOVERED EMPTY, two men walked along the road to Emmaus and discussed what had happened. Jesus approached them and walked with them for several miles. They did not recognize Jesus, and they were surprised that he had not heard the big news. Jesus spoke prophetically to them, but it wasn't until he broke bread with them that they recognized him as the risen Lord. Then they departed to share with the other disciples that they had encountered Jesus.

In 2017, I had the great gift of undertaking a walking pilgrimage with fellow University of Notre Dame alumni. Over fourteen days, we covered three hundred miles, retracing the steps Rev. Edward Sorin, C.S.C., and his brother priests took in the year 1842 when they departed Vincennes, Indiana, to found the university in South Bend. Our journey together began long before those two weeks traversing Indiana in August: We trained for more than a year, virtually praying with and for one another and our campus community.

Training for and walking the Notre Dame Trail forever changed my attitude about walking. The Trail was meant to commemorate the 175th anniversary of the university, but each pilgrim had their own motivation. Mine was to discern the path ahead of me during a time of personal transition. While we never lacked conversation along the trail, I savored those moments when silence enveloped me. I often prayed over the passage from Luke's Gospel where two men unknowingly walked alongside the risen Jesus for seven miles. I thought many times during the twelve months I spent living the Trail about what I would say to Jesus if I'd been on that road to Emmaus.

I love walking. While I walk for exercise, I never hesitate to slow my pace to notice a blooming flower, a perched bird, or a perfect view. I walk solo most days, but I love it when a family member or friend walks beside me. The miles float by as the conversation flows. The Notre Dame Trail did not conclude for me when we crossed the finish line after having traversed hundreds of miles. For me, that was in many ways simply the start of my journey. Since the Trail, I have understood that I never walk alone. Regardless of where my path takes me, Jesus walks alongside me. Part of the joy of walking now is keeping my eyes and heart open so that I recognize him along the path. He is no doubt there.

My Sunday Reflection

How can I open my eyes and heart to recognize Jesus in disguise?

MONDAY

> The soul that walks in love neither tires others nor grows tired.

ST. JOHN OF THE CROSS,
THE COLLECTED WORKS OF ST. JOHN OF THE CROSS

Where can I seek rest in Jesus along my daily journey?

TUESDAY

> Indeed, that is the charm about Christ, when all is said: he is just like a work of art. He does not really teach one anything, but by being brought into his presence one becomes something. And everybody is predestined to his presence. Once at least in his life each man walks with Christ to Emmaus.

OSCAR WILDE, *DE PROFUNDIS*

When have I knowingly walked with Jesus?

WEDNESDAY

> When on my country walks I go,
> I never am alone:
> Though whom 'twere pleasure then to know
> Are gone, and you are gone;
> From every side discourses flow.

HERBERT P. HORNE, "AMICO SUO"

What helps me know that Jesus is with me?

THURSDAY

> I am alarmed when it happens that I have walked a mile into the woods bodily, without getting there in spirit.
>
> HENRY DAVID THOREAU, *WALKING*

How can I set aside my distractions and worries?

FRIDAY

> Try and be nice to people, avoid eating fat, read a good book every now and then, get some walking in, and try and live together in peace and harmony with people of all creeds and nations.
>
> *MONTY PYTHON'S THE MEANING OF LIFE*

Where can I fit more walking with Jesus into my life?

SATURDAY

> Thus says the LORD:
> Stand by the crossroads, and look,
> and ask for the ancient paths,
> where the good way lies; and walk in it,
> and find rest for your souls.
> But they said, "We will not walk in it."
>
> JEREMIAH 6:16

How am I trying to walk in the good way, mindful of Jesus walking alongside me?

Let us pray.

Jesus, you walked alongside Cleopas and his friend on their journey to Emmaus.

While your words and presence inspired them, it wasn't until you broke bread with them that they knew it was you.

Accompany me, Jesus, so that every path leads me closer to you.

Open my heart, Lord, to recognize you with every step.

Amen.

WEEK 52

SUNDAY

Following Jesus

Peter Is Given a Command—John 21:15–19

He said to him the third time, "Simon, son of John, do you love me?" Peter felt hurt because he said to him the third time, "Do you love me?" And he said to him, "Lord, you know everything; you know that I love you." Jesus said to him, "Feed my sheep. Very truly, I tell you, when you were younger, you used to fasten your own belt and to go wherever you wished. But when you grow old, you will stretch out your hands, and someone else will fasten a belt around you and take you where you do not wish to go." (He said this to indicate the kind of death by which he would glorify God.) And after this he said to him, "Follow me."

JOHN 21:17–19

AFTER JESUS HAD FINISHED having breakfast with his disciples, he spoke directly to Simon Peter. Three times, Jesus asked Peter, "Do you love me?" Three times, Peter assured Jesus he did, and the Lord gave him directives, saying, "Feed my lambs," "Tend my sheep," and "Feed my sheep." Then, Jesus told Peter what lay ahead and finished with two simple words: *Follow me.*

Follow me. The words sound so simple, don't they? In his post-breakfast conversation with Peter, Jesus questioned him three times about his love. Peter, growing impatient, assured him three times that he did. After each proclamation of love, Jesus asked Simon Peter to undertake tasks that would prove his love. These three interactions echo Peter's three denials of Jesus, spoken only days before.

The mission Jesus gave Peter was one not meant for a blind follower. Instead, he set Peter up as a shepherd, reminding him that loving meant caring for those Jesus had gathered unto himself. Just like Peter, you and I are asked, by our discipleship, not just to say, "I love you," but to live those words daily. Following Jesus doesn't just mean we are doing this for ourselves. It means embracing the love he showers upon us and then pouring it into everyone we meet.

We feed his lambs—our families and friends—literally and figuratively by sharing our gifts.

We tend his sheep by giving our attention to them, listening to them, and leading them into safety and security. We feed his sheep with the most incredible sustenance we have from Jesus—his body and blood, given for each of us out of love.

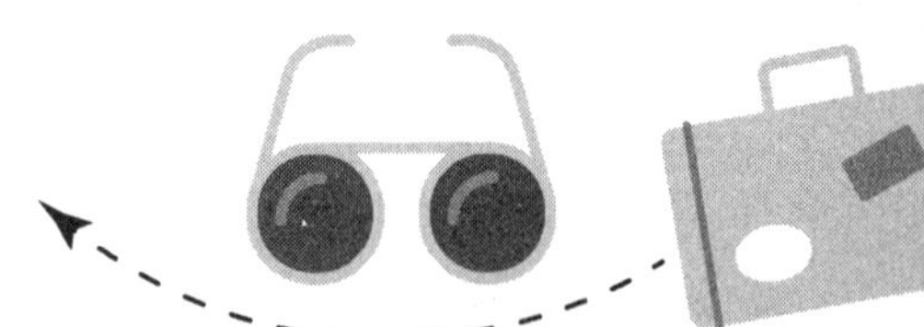

"You know everything, Lord! You know that I love you." How many times have I verbally professed these words only to contradict them by my actions? Truly following Jesus is a daily choice and one undertaken with foreknowledge of how difficult the path ahead can be. But our fellow sheep, those we are asked to feed and tend, do the same for us. We each lead, follow, tend and are tended, and are followed and fed. Our love for Jesus and for one another points us to the path we are called to follow, which leads us into all that he promises—and more.

And so we follow, one small step at a time.

My Sunday Reflection

How is Jesus asking me to follow him?

MONDAY

God did not make the first human because he needed company, but because he wanted someone to whom he could show his generosity and love. God did not tell us to follow him because he needed our help, but because he knew that loving him would make us whole.

ST. IRENAEUS

When has knowing that I am loved made following Jesus easier for me?

TUESDAY

It is to the Cross that the Christian is challenged to follow his Master: no path of redemption can make a detour around it.

HANS URS VON BALTHASAR, *UNLESS YOU BECOME LIKE THIS CHILD*

What cross am I asked to take up to follow Jesus lovingly?

WEDNESDAY

I love thee with a love I seemed to lose
With my lost saints. I love thee with the breath,
Smiles, tears, of all my life; and, if God choose,
I shall but love thee better after death.

ELIZABETH BARRETT BROWNING,
"HOW DO I LOVE THEE? (SONNET 43)"

How am I striving every day to love Jesus with more of myself?

THURSDAY

> In reality, to know the Lord, it is not enough to know something about Him, but rather to follow Him, to let oneself be touched and changed by His Gospel. It is a matter of having a relationship with Him, an encounter.

POPE FRANCIS, ANGELUS, SEPTEMBER 15, 2024

How is Jesus inviting me into a more profound encounter with him?

FRIDAY

> You are my friends. And there is no greater love than for a man to lay down his life for his friends. I cannot be with you much longer, my friends. You cannot go where I am going. My commandment to you after I am gone is this: Love one another. As I have loved you, so love one another.

THE PASSION OF THE CHRIST

Who are my friends? Am I loving, feeding, and tending to them as Jesus asks?

SATURDAY

> My sheep hear my voice. I know them, and they follow me. I give them eternal life, and they will never perish. No one shall snatch them out of my hand.

JOHN 10:27–28

Where have I heard Jesus's voice calling me to follow him? How did I reply?

Let us pray.

Jesus, just as you asked Peter to express
and to live his love for you, you ask me,
"Do you love me?"

Lord, you know that I love you, even when my
humanity and brokenness might say otherwise.

Be patient with me. Instill in me the grit,
perseverance, and compassion to follow
you and tend to and feed those you have
entrusted to me.

I love you, Jesus, and I will follow wherever
you lead.

Amen.

Acknowledgments

Perhaps it's fitting that as I pen the first draft of my acknowledgments for this work, a rideshare driver named Dante is safely ferrying me through rush hour traffic toward downtown Chicago. The Peruvian tunes Dante blasts on the stereo bridge our linguistic barrier. We both work hard at our occupations while at the same time we share bits of our stories. While Dante is simply one of the many people I've met while working on this book, I will remember him and many others as new friends who helped me put my screen down, open my eyes and my heart, and listen closely to the whispers Jesus is sending my way, often in unexpected places like the backseat of an Uber. To every person whose story is shared here: Thank you for being a part of my journey and for helping me know Jesus more fully through how you live and who you are.

When acknowledging the many people who help a book to be born, it feels fitting to begin with my fantastic team at Loyola Press. Most specifically, I am grateful to Gary Jansen, whose outreach in spring 2024 opened my heart and mind to this excellent topic. Alongside Gary, my editor Maura Poston offered such a lovely perspective to these pages. Maura, thank you for the emergency help in a moment of panic and all the everyday writing adventures in between. To the remainder of the Loyola team, including production manager Donna Antkowiak, copyeditor Susan Taylor, proofreader Alison Shurtz, and design professionals Carrie Schuler, who created the front cover, and Kathryn Seckman, who crafted the back cover and the book's engaging interior, thank you for helping my words look so good.

Writers benefit from a lifetime of formation. Specifically, I wish to thank the educational institutions that formed my mind, heart, body, and soul. To St. Barbara's School, Sr. Colette Walter and the Sisters of St. Francis of the Neumann Communities, Mater Dei High School, the College of Arts and Letters at the University of Notre Dame, and Peabody College at Vanderbilt University: Thank you for the many lessons you taught me inside and outside your classrooms.

To my support communities, including my faith family at St. Paul the Apostle Catholic Community in Los Angeles, my Women's Faith Sharing friends, my online community of writing colleagues, and my Holy Cross Family Ministries, Family Theater Productions, and CatholicMom.com family: Thank you for praying for me through these pages. To my buddies in the UCLA Volunteer Department and the amazing women of the UCLA Auxiliary: Thank you for allowing me to work in your company and for the powerful service you offer to so many.

This work was undertaken during my treatment for breast cancer. I remain forever grateful to my caregiving team at UCLA Health for helping me heal in all areas of my life, and to the Cancer Support Community of Los Angeles for being a neighborhood of healing support and compassion.

Mom and Daddy, thank you for your many heavenly assists and for sowing the seeds of faith in my heart from day one. To my "B Sibs" Erin, Patrick, Brady, and Michael, as well as your partners and my incredible niece and nephews, words can never express what the gift of our family means to me. Thank you to the extended Hendey family for claiming me as your daughter, sister, aunt, and friend.

To Eric, Lea, Adam, Frannie, Charlotte, Sophia, and the precious grandbaby whose birth we now await, my incredible family: Thank you for teaching me to see our world from many new and wonderful perspectives. Being your mom and grandma is the most powerful gift in my life.

To Greg: You are my "why," and the reason I wake up each day with a heart filled with love, joy, and hope. Thank you for your encouragement to continue chasing my dreams, and for taking care of me in good times and in challenging ones, too. I witness your love for Jesus in how you love and care for me. I can't wait to see where our adventure takes us next. Wherever that may be, it's perfect to know that we will journey together always.

To God, my heavenly Father, to Jesus Christ who accompanies me every step, and to the Holy Spirit who lights the way, be all glory forever.

About the Author

Lisa M. Hendey is the founder of CatholicMom.com and the bestselling author of several books for adults and children, including *The Grace of Yes*, *The Catholic Mom's Prayer Companion*, and *I'm a Saint in the Making*. Lisa's children's project, the Chime Travelers fiction series for elementary school readers, which dynamically combines time travel and the lives of the saints, is read in schools, children's groups, and churches worldwide. It is now streaming as an animated series.

The host of the "Lisa Hendey & Friends" podcast, Lisa has produced and hosted multiple programs and has appeared on EWTN, CNN, CatholicTV, and various radio outlets. Her articles have appeared in *Catholic Digest*, *America Magazine*, *National Catholic Register*, and *Our Sunday Visitor*.

Hendey travels internationally, giving workshops and retreats. She was selected as an Elizabeth Egan Journalism Fellow. Lisa has traveled and shared her writing from Rwanda, Tanzania, Colombia, the Philippines, Kenya, the Dominican Republic, Australia, and India to serve several nonprofit organizations and share their messages of hope and service.

Lisa M. Hendey is ready to share her insights with your group. She is available to speak on a variety of topics, including faith, family, work-life balance, cancer survivorship, and healthy living.

For more information about Lisa Hendey and her work, visit her website at www.LisaHendey.com. You can also connect with her on social media at @LisaHendey. Lisa and her husband Greg are active members of the Archdiocese of Los Angeles, California.

Fonts do so much to give a book its signature look and feel. In creating the interior of *Jesus Every Day, Jesus Every Way*, we selected a range of typefaces that balance readability with elegance.

Adobe Garamond Pro, a revival of the classic sixteenth-century type by Claude Garamond, lends a timeless literary feel to the body text. Helvetica Neue, with its clean, modern lines, adds clarity and contrast in headings and captions. Celestia Antiqua offers a refined, classical aesthetic rooted in Roman letterforms, while Abril Display brings a contemporary serif flair to the page.

Together, these fonts reflect Lisa Hendey's warm hospitality, inviting the reader into a thoughtfully designed spiritual experience.